ACCENTED
FUTURES

ACCENTED FUTURES

Language Activism and the Ending of Apartheid

CARLI COETZEE

WITS UNIVERSITY PRESS

Published in South Africa by:

Wits University Press
1 Jan Smuts Avenue
Johannesburg

www.witspress.co.za

First published 2013

ISBN 978-1-86814-740-3 (print)
ISBN 978-1-86814-741-0 (digital)

Cover photograph and page 63 by Thembinkosi Goniwe, courtesy of Iziko
Photograph page 24 by Antjie Krog, courtesy of UKZN Press
Photograph bottom of page 63 by Nick Aldridge
Photographs pages 112, 119 and 120 by Max Edkins

Edited by Monica Seeber
Cover design and layout by Hothouse South Africa
Printed and bound by Interpak Books

CONTENTS

To my students, and to my children

Acknowledgements

For early encouragement and the conversations that influenced this book, I thank Silvia Elsner, Loyiso Nongxa, Manuela Vogel and Liese van der Watt. Lindiwe Dovey has been a constant interlocutor for this work, and her stimulating conversations and challenging interventions are everywhere inscribed in its pages. To the members of the Department of Languages and Cultures of Africa at SOAS in London, thank you for inviting me in and for providing me with an intellectual home outside South Africa. To my students at SOAS, and to the students I taught in South Africa, thank you for the most challenging and exciting exchanges anyone could ever imagine, or hope for.

Thank you to Derek Attridge, Brenda Cooper, Jacob Dlamini, Kai Easton, Patrick Flanery, Pumla Gqola, Thembinkosi Goniwe, Wandile Kasibe, Kgomotso Masemola, Sarah Nuttall, Tlhalo Raditlhalo, Mark Sanders, Pam Scully, Hedley Twidle, Andrew van der Vlies, Liese van der Watt and Lindy Wilbraham for their comments on earlier drafts of sections of this book; to Jacques Coetzee and Meg Samuelson for agreeing to read it all, and for their valuable comments. Thank you to the anonymous reviewers, in particular to 'Reader 3', for useful advice and criticism. Chandré Carstens went to look for the post office stones and the post shoe, and sent me photographs and descriptions. My Xhosa grammar teachers, Pam Maseko and Tessa Dowling, gave me advice on verb forms; Motlatsi Mabaso and Matshabello Sannah Mokone were generous with their time to view and discuss the Sotho conversations in 'Ask Me, I'm Positive'. Lutz Marten offered early enthusiastic support, and talked through the issues around the naming of languages. Thank you also to my South African literature teachers, and in particular to the first real teacher I ever had (and who has remained the measure of all teachers since then), Sue Marais, who lent me a copy of *In the Heart of the Country* to read and trusted me to make meaning of it.

Thank you to my colleagues in the English Departments at the University of the Western Cape and the University of Cape Town, for conversations and companionship, and to the WEB du Bois Institute at Harvard University, for hosting me so generously in 1999-2000 and again in 2011. The first work towards this book was completed there, a long time ago now.

Thanks also to Thembinkosi Goniwe for allowing me to reproduce his art work on the book cover; to Don, Max and Teboho Edkins for their images and comments, and to UKZN Press for the image from *There was this Goat*. Wits University Press have been a real pleasure to work with, and Monica Seeber the editor an author can only dream to have.

And to Mark, Harriet and Joseph: thank you for everything.

Preface

Some time ago, a student at SOAS, the School of Oriental and African Studies in London, asked me, in a class on South African writing: 'So when *did* apartheid end?', meaning when were the first democratic elections held. Or, perhaps, when was grand apartheid dismantled and taken off the statute books? Or, subliminally, in response to commemorations of the twentieth anniversary of the day, when did the world see Nelson Mandela walk free? All of these could be provided as answers, but instead I wanted to say: 'Has it?' This may seem like a pessimistic response, but I want to frame it differently. Apartheid is end*ing* (even if one may want to insist, as I do, that it has not ended), and there is a crucial place for academic writing and teaching in this process of the long ending and new beginning. In the reluctance to accept an easy 'post' position for South Africa (post-apartheid, post-race) my intention is not to diminish what has been achieved already, but instead to contribute to developing ways of thinking forward, and modes of writing, reading and teaching that are actively and positively engaged in the further work of this ending.

My understanding of this enduring ending is not the one to be found in the kind of writing and thinking arguing that South Africa is post-apartheid (and therefore history has become irrelevant, the 'post' erasing the responsibilities and formations of the past). Nor is it the kind of ending that chooses to be silenced and to perform this silence as proof that a certain kind of voice, a certain kind of opinion, is 'finished', the time for it over. There is also another kind of talk about endings with which I do not want to agree, which says that apartheid may have ended but nothing has changed, that the 'post-ness' is somehow fake. Perhaps what ties together these senses of the ending is the expectation that the end will be finite, that there will have been a morning when the world woke up to a new day that bore no traces of what had gone before.

In this book's interpretation of the long ending of the previous time, the time when apartheid was inscribed (asymmetrically, diversely) in and on much of South Africans' lives, the ending is understood as an activity, and as a point of view that needs to be developed and cultivated. I call this work 'accenting'. The way in which I use the term 'accented' in this book is to refer to ways of thinking that are aware of the legacies of the past, and do not attempt to empty out the conflicts and violence under the surface. Accented thinking and accented conversations will often, perhaps typically, appear conflictual and overly insistent on difference and disagreement. In this book I argue that it is precisely those discourses that *acknowledge* the asymmetrical legacies of apartheid, and draw attention to the enduring effects of the violent past, that can bring about the long ending of apartheid.

The value of this accented sense of an ending is that it requires a regard for the past and a responsibility to seek out that about which one *chooses* not to be ignorant. It is an understanding of the sense of the ending of apartheid as an activist task in which there is work to be done: precisely the work towards this ending. In other words, it is not enough to uphold the ideal of nonracialism through merely *stating* it ('apartheid has ended'). That position requires constant work; and work that will require a high degree of tolerance for disagreement and discord. This activist work – which includes academic writing and teaching, but is not only that – is a way of countering discourses of failure and disappointment, and of reversing a potential paralysis and silence.

My argument here insists on the necessity of acquiring particular kinds of knowledge about the South African past and present as a way of making a different future. This book aims to reach a general audience, and not only those with the interests and conventions of academic writing in mind. Yet higher education is a major concern in the book, and the university provides the backdrop for a number of the chapters. The university is at times the physical location of a research project or an artwork that I discuss. Sometimes it is the staff common room or the library that sets the scene for one of the discordant encounters I analyse. Throughout the book, learning and teaching encounters are scrutinised for what they reveal about power relations and who the beneficiaries are of knowledge and scholarship. In this book I am often suspicious of teaching situations, and of the ways in which scholarship can maintain exclusive circuits of prestige and gain. In the accented pursuit of knowledge, I argue, it is not the student alone who needs to be transformed, but also the teacher and the teaching institution. This book offers a theorisation of the teaching and learning encounter that is insistent on the self-transforming labour to be performed by teachers and teaching institutions.

The arguments of this book return to questions of divided audiences and to conversation partners who are in conflict over the meanings of their encounters. The subjects chosen for analysis present versions of 'accented' discourse: conversations and encounters that are often marked by disagreement and disappointment. They do not speak in monolingual voices (even if the encounter is written in one language only). The definition of a South African accent is one that insists on the multiplicity of this accent. In fact, the defining characteristic of this accented thinking is that it is not spoken in just one accent, but instead represents an orientation that creates an awareness of and an 'ear' for many and diverse accents, and for the diverse forms of knowledge and languages around us. While the argument returns to the question of apartheid, and to South Africanness, it may well be that these questions do not remain as pertinent to a next generation as they are to my own. Younger readers of the material, or readers elsewhere, may well find its insistence on South Africanness perplexing and even counter-productive. And it may in fact be a good thing for the times to outgrow the concern of this work with apartheid, with exclusion and transformation. Integral to the work outlined in this book is a tolerance for difference and disagreement, and a willingness to show vulnerability at the same time as taking up resistant and challenging positions. I call these approaches and orientations 'accented thinking'.

I argue for the preference of accent over translation as a way of understanding activist reading and teaching practices, and the book often makes arguments *against* translation – or at least translation of a particular kind. Translation has often been held up as a benevolent metaphor for imagining and learning the position of others. But when the relationship between the languages involved is unequal, I argue, translation can strengthen the inherited inequalities in society. Therefore this book makes an argument against translation in contexts where being 'understood' is not to the advantage of the speaker. Resisting translation, and being misunderstood, can be powerful tools for bringing about transformation. Such instances of challenging and deliberately difficult discourses are what I regard as ideally 'accented'.

Translation may have provided me with a rather more positive way of theorising these encounters, and translation is a common enough metaphor for acknowledging and even foregrounding difference. Translation always involves an awareness of audience, and the two (or more) contexts (language and culture) of the text's reception. In addition, translation, like the accentedness I theorise about, builds on the many insights of scholars of orality, for whom context and audience are key elements of an utterance's meanings. Accented reading and teaching practices, like translations, are invested in the particular encounter and the particular kinds of knowledge held by an audience; but also in the intertextual references that an audience brings to a work.

There is an important difference between translation and accented thinking, however, and that is accent's additional emphasis on unacknowledged power inequalities and on conflict and disagreement. In this way, accent (rather than translation) provides me with a framework that allows for keeping apartheid's histories and legacies prominent, without having to accept apartheid's insistence on skin and surface. Accent is also a better concept for another reason: it allows for more resistant and transformative positions; positions insistent on precisely *not* translating oneself in someone else's terms. A number of chapters analyse the gains of accented discourse as well as the gains of learning to hear and speak in accented ways.

Chapter 1 theorises accent, and provides a framework arguing in favour of disagreement and conflict in discourse as a way of doing the activist work of ending apartheid. In Chapter 2, I introduce ideas on the ethics of learning and teaching by looking at an example of a collaborative multilingual project which examines the conditions necessary for learning to take place. The chapter offers a reading of *There Was This Goat*, a book which aims to see what a difference a respectful and situated translation can make to the words of someone who is not a powerful person. The book is the product of excavating the meanings of the words of a grieving mother to the Truth and Reconciliation Commission. In this chapter I pay attention to the university as locus of the research project and to the advantage of this research work; in the chapters that follow, the ideas and arguments return to the classroom, the staff common room, and the library – but also to the places the student and teacher come from.

In the third chapter I read Njabulo Ndebele's essays with an eye for comments on the hegemony of English and the ways in which conversational discourses in South Africa are skewed by unacknowledged hierarchies. This chapter reflects on translation, and the inequalities of the translational encounter. In Ndebele's work there is a strand of thinking that unsettles and dislodges the dominance of English and its associated power. It is not only English as a language that bars certain speakers or precludes utterances, but also the histories and tastes associated with what 'English' (English departments, the teaching of English, the English Academy) represents. Read like this, Ndebele's theorisation of ordinariness in his article 'Rediscovery of the Ordinary' takes on a strong political significance, as a way of thinking about how we can *become* ordinary. I argue that this ordinariness will be marked by disagreement and the acknowledgment of differences of opinion. Ndebele's work includes a strand of distrust and insistence on misunderstanding, and these resistant positions provide clear examples of accented discourse and thinking.

In the fourth chapter, I develop ideas of resistance and accent further. This chapter examines an instance of *performed* non-understanding, through the reading of an artwork, 'Returning the gaze' by Thembinkosi Goniwe, which is partly a self-portrait. I argue that Goniwe unsettles the viewer, positioning her in a place where she is made to acknowledge (or *forced to assume* the position of someone who does so) her difference, and her non-neutrality. The artwork forces the viewer to 'perform', uncomfortably, the role of someone refusing to meet the gaze of the artist in his self-portrait. In this chapter I develop the idea that construing, performing even, being misunderstood can be a powerful tool in unsettling certainties. This is different to the way in which language has so often been seen, in recent South African discourses, as a tool for reconciliation and unification. In the argument in this chapter, insistence on disagreement and the acknowledgment of misunderstanding (rather than resolution and harmony) are held up as productively resistant positions.

The fifth chapter develops my ideas on sceptical approaches to translation. I use a rather literal interpretation of the term 'address', as the chapter examines actual letters and the addresses to where they are to be sent. I look at the early written texts that document the colonial encounter (letters and reports written by seventeenth-century European merchants and travellers from and about what we now call the South African landscape), showing that these early texts, even when they are literally inscribed on the landscape, on rocks and trees, precisely are *not* addressed to a 'local' reader, and nor do the meanings of these texts aim to bring any gain to the 'local' context. The concerns of this chapter, then, are with the location of the gains and benefits to be derived from knowledge, and it uses the history of translation as a practice in South Africa to ask to what extent translation in the early Cape can be read as an intertextual and contextual practice. My argument is that it functions precisely *not* as a form of intertextuality, and in this sense provides us with an early history of *lack* of inter-lingual communication. In this chapter I want to demythologise translation as a metaphor for greater understanding and identification, and to draw attention instead to translation's silencing effects and to the enduring effects of early translation practices in South Africa.

Translation is concerned with bringing the meanings of the original text and its contexts into other languages and contexts. The notion of origin and original has been questioned from many theoretical perspectives, including translation theory.

What the next chapter does is to look at a particular example of translated work, where the originals no longer exist and the 'translated' version circulates as a new original. This chapter examines the writings and markings left on the land by the early rock painters and markers of the landscape. Some of the original artworks have fallen out of circulation, been deleted, or have otherwise been removed. In some cases this is because fragile rock art has been destroyed or has decayed naturally; but my argument is that the lost original is not incidental to the ways in which these transcribed, 'translated' artworks and texts have come to be known. In the place of the (lost) artworks comes to stand academic scholarship, claiming its own place as the 'origin'. Linked to this is a common desire by scholars of these early works to present their scholarship as benevolent histories and archives. The chapter reflects on this urge, and its implications for the ethics of our knowledge. I read the recurring concern with the notion of copies and originals as, possibly, an expression of anxiety around the unspoken theft that haunts South African thought – the theft of the land.

The seventh chapter develops the theme of teaching as ideally an accented practice. It examines two examples of the ideal teacher – one taken from the HIV/Aids educational 'STEPS for the Future' films, the other from Jonny Steinberg's book *Three Letter Plague*. In the STEPS films, we see teachers who are responsive to context and whose ethics of teaching lead them (and us) to examine our relationship to knowledge. In Jonny Steinberg's book, the informant/teacher chooses to remain anonymous. This encypherment provides a lens through which I read Steinberg's book, and analyse the ways in which it imagines its own readers and their relationship to what has been documented. At issue is the ownership of the story, and the authorship not only of the book but of the meanings of the teacher's (Sizwe's) life. Steinberg develops an argument that allows the reader to think of illness and medicine as languages; and through Sizwe's words we come to see how ARV drugs speak the 'wrong' language, and are not trusted by ordinary, local men (and women, but Steinberg's text is not so interested in them). In Sizwe, the argument goes, we see another version of the teacher, with Steinberg as his pupil. But in Steinberg's book we see also the unequal relationship Steinberg and his teacher have to knowledge and to English. In this chapter, then, questions of translation are brought to bear on the classroom, and I show the ambiguities around the position of those I describe as 'ideal' teachers.

Chapter 8 continues the analysis of the asymmetrical relations that South Africans have always had to language and to knowledge. This is done by way of a reading of *Native Nostalgia*, in which Jacob Dlamini's historiographical project is to develop the appropriate senses (and the intellectual tools to excavate them) to write about the 'ordinary' lives and the tastes of South Africans. The argument highlights, in particular, his reflections on the uses of the Afrikaans language by black South Africans. Dlamini writes of his mother and her peers speaking Afrikaans to one another, imbuing the language with 'ordinary' meanings, over and above the meanings Afrikaans has had, especially to those speakers of the language who claim ownership of it. In this ordinary use there is an example of the accented reading practice this book outlines, in the sense that the speakers of Afrikaans in this chapter are making their own meanings that alter the dominant understandings of their lives and their words. The value of Dlamini's work lies in his theorisation of the search for new archives, and in this way it can be read as an attempt at writing accented histories of South Africa. In his writing about Afrikaans, he provides a striking example of the complex forms of resistance that can be articulated through accented speech.

In Chapter 9 the location of the accented reader is theorised through a reading of some of the fictional and critical work of the South African-born writer Zoë Wicomb. Wicomb's writing returns often to the question of address in the sense of geographical location (that of her characters as well as their author). In this chapter I reflect on how and whether it is possible to theorise and adopt a South African accent when living elsewhere – and show that of course the converse is true too, that it is possible to live an unaccented life anywhere. Wicomb writes about the reading practices of the reader who reads provincially or locally (I would call it accentedly) in the first place; and this is illustrated by a reading of Wicomb's own work as well as an analysis of an unauthorised (but published) interview with her, in which questions of location and the meanings of 'home' feature prominently. This chapter concludes with a section in which I wilfully attempt an accented reading of a small selection of the works of JM Coetzee, perhaps the South African author whose works circulate in the least accented ways.

Chapter 10 offers a rather personal reflection on teaching and accentedness. It is influenced by the writing of scholars on pedagogy, in particular Jane Gallop's work *Anecdotal Theory* and her edited collection *Pedagogy: The Question of Impersonation.* In this chapter I attempt to reflect on my own accented practices, as well as on their ambiguities and failures. But the chapter does not dismiss these accounts of failures; it speculates on the miscommunications and misreadings in particular classrooms and teaching encounters, and offers a theorisation of teaching as an accented practice.

This book reflects on the forms of resistance, and on versions of activism. I argue for understanding the conflicts and failures in many of the chapters as instances of what James C Scott describes as the 'rupture' when that which has had to remain hidden is finally spoken. In this way, then, the conflicts and disagreements in the book are presented as instances of the ending of apartheid although, at the same time, the Conclusion tempers a too celebratory tone, as there is an acknowledgment of the losses and silences of South Africa's histories, and the need to excavate and to conserve the many accented versions of the past.

A NOTE ON TERMINOLOGY

I have chosen in this book to refer to the many South African languages by their 'English' names. So I write Xhosa, not isiXhosa. There are good arguments for writing isiXhosa, which indicates one's awareness of the noun classes of the language, and that a word like Xhosa can belong to a class which shows that the word describes a person, or a language, or a book. Some would also argue that it is a sign of respect to use the prefix. My own position is that using the prefix, while writing in English, implies an exaggerated and false sense of including languages other than English.

Chapter 1

AGAINST TRANSLATION, IN DEFENCE OF ACCENTEDNESS

AGAINST TRANSLATION

Translation would seem to offer much to someone imagining a future different from the apartheid past: it emphasises mutuality, is intent on contextualisation and demands of one to imagine the position of another. Yet in the following pages I make a number of arguments *against* translation. I show why I prefer accentedness to translation as a description of the activist work of the ending of apartheid, and argue that refusal to translate or resistance to being translated are forms of the activism this book analyses and theorises.

There is a growing literature from within translation studies that is suspicious of itself and of its own good intentions. Translation, Susan Bassnett has written, can be understood as 'an effect of inequalities' (2002: 4) rather than as a meeting of equals. In this version of translation work, it can be seen as a suspect activity in which inequalities (of economics, politics, gender, geography) are not only reflected but also reproduced in the mechanics of textual production. Bassnett summarises:

> Perhaps the most exciting new trend of all is the expansion of the discipline of translation studies beyond the boundaries of Europe … More emphasis has been placed on the inequality of the translation relationship with writers such as Gayatri Chakravorty Spivak, Tejaswini Niranjana and Eric Cheyfitz arguing that translation was effectively used in the past as an instrument of colonial domination, a means of depriving the colonised peoples of a voice. For in the colonial model, one culture dominated and the others were subservient, hence translation reinforced that power hierarchy (Bassnett 2002: 4).

The insight that translation features in asymmetrical relations is not new. In a 1986 paper on 'The Concept of Cultural Translation in British Social Anthropology', Talal Asad had this to say on the inequality of languages: 'I have proposed that the anthropological enterprise of cultural translation may be vitiated by the fact that there are asymmetrical tendencies and pressures in the languages of dominated and dominant societies. And I have suggested that anthropologists need to explore these processes in order to determine how far they go in defining the possibilities and the limits of effective translation' (1986: 164). This line of inquiry has been taken up in another context by Tejaswini Niranjana in *Siting Translation: History, Post-Structuralism, and the Colonial Context*: 'Translation as a practice shapes, and takes shape within, the asymmetrical relations of power that operate under colonialism' (1992: 2). Niranjana (1992: 84) argues that it is possible for bilingual translators to 'challenge earlier Western versions through retranslation' – to think here of translation as an act of resistance and self-representation. I develop these ideas in this book, and argue that the act of *refusing* to translate, or to be translated, can be a powerful form of resistance. It is a truism that resisting translation runs the risk that it can be confused with silence – and the complications around the reputed silence of the 'subaltern' have received a great deal of attention.

Niranjana concludes her book by writing:

> since post-colonials already exist 'in translation', our search should not be for origins or essences but for a richer complexity, a complication of our notions of the 'self', a more densely textured understanding of who 'we' are. It is here that translators can intervene to inscribe heterogeneity, to warn against myths of purity, to show origins as always already fissured. Translation, from being a 'containing' force, is transformed into a disruptive, disseminating one. The deconstruction initiated by re-translation opens up a post-colonial space as it brings 'history to legibility' (1992: 186).

What this means here is clear: the postcolonial translator (or re-translator) has to resist the homogenised (orientalised, some might say as a shorthand) representations of ourselves/themselves, and offer, instead, heterogeneity and a refusal of essence. This same insistence on heterogeniety is found in debates around varieties of English. Like English elsewhere in Africa (and a vast literature exists around this – see the edited collection by Rajend Mesthrie, *Language in South Africa*, 2002, for an overview of the scholarship), its identities and uses are complex. The version of translation studies outlined in Niranjana's work can lead, for South African English, to the disruption of the myth of colonial origin and language purity (see also Rajend Mesthrie's recent *Eish But is it English? Celebrating the South African Variety*, 2011).

This in turn means that English is viewed as diverse and accented *within* itself, a reorientation that is theorised in Njabulo Ndebele's work. Ndebele shows that what may seem like an openness to the different versions (and accents, my book would add) of English may in the end turn out to be an attempt at benign containment by those keen to keep English 'standard' – that is, unaccented. Linked to this risk of containment, or accent loss, is also the question of translation out of African language texts and into English. One might argue for the importance of disseminating more widely texts that are written in African languages; yet translation out of African languages into English can also become a form of containment, a deletion of the accents of the text. In addition, the labour of translation risks remaining invisible, the smoothness of the English-language translation replacing the original utterance, which becomes over-inscribed with the new translated version, rendering the original (in this case the African language text or document) invisibly contained.

In this version of translation, the burden of labour falls on those who speak languages other than English; that burden is to translate into English, allowing English to remain the standard and the norm. This might also allow monolingual English speakers to remain monolingual, benefiting from the work of those who translate. In her essay (or rather the English language translation) 'Consecration and accumulation of literary capital: Translation as unequal exchange', Pascale Casanova writes: 'Far from being the horizontal exchange and peaceful transfer often described, translation must be understood, on the contrary, as an "unequal exchange" that takes place in a strongly hierarchised universe' (2009: 86). Casanova is mostly interested in the role translation can play in the consecration of authors and texts, and how literary 'capital' is generated and transferred through the work of translation. My interest is not so much in the status of the texts and authors as 'capital', but rather in the work of translation, the *labour*, itself.

Recent work on interpreting and witnessing in war and conflict situations has much to offer us in this resistant understanding of translation. In *The Translation Zone*, Emily Apter (2006) pays attention to metaphors of war and regionality, and wants to bring to the surface the potential political meanings of translation and its limits:

> The book aims to rethink translation studies – a field traditionally defined by problems of linguistic and textual fidelity to the original – in a broad theoretical framework that emphasises the role played by mistranslation in war, the influence of language and literature wars on canon formation and literary fields, the aesthetic significance of experiments with nonstandard language ... (2006: 3).

Apter is also interested in what she terms 'nontranslation, mistranslation, and the disputed translation of evidentiary visual information'. Mistranslation here refers to 'a concrete particular of the art of war, crucial to strategy and tactics, part and parcel of the way in which images of bodies are read ... It is also the name of diplomatic breakdown and paranoid misreading' (2006: 15). For Apter, it would be accurate to regard war as, in fact, 'a condition of nontranslatability or translation failure at its most violent peak' (2006: 16).

In the South African context, the Truth and Reconciliation Commission (TRC) and the way its work has been reported provide a fascinating example of such a translation failure. Some might argue that the Truth and Reconciliation Commission is the opposite of war, a commission that has as its intention the unification of a nation after civil war. Yet insisting on mistranslation and non-translatability has been one strand in the critical response to the TRC. Understanding, in this version, risks containment; for to understand means to forgive. For an illustration of the effects of a refusal to forgive, one may think of Nkosinathi Biko's resistance (2000: 193-8) to the TRC process. The literature on the TRC is vast (some useful academic responses include Posel and Simpson's, Villa Vicenzio's and Wilson's), but I want here to highlight just one aspect of this literature, what Apter might call 'translation failure'. I am interested, in particular, in the ways in which this translation failure can be interpreted as a form of accented resistance. Failure to translate, in this argument, can be read as resistance to be included in a particular version of the past.

Debates around the TRC also provide excellent examples of the ways in which translation into English is not neutral, and in which the direction of translation itself has a history. Interpreters and translators laboured to translate the testimonies of victims and survivors into English, the translated version being taken up as the *official* version. Richard Wilson's (2001) chapter 'Technologies of truth: The TRC's truth-making machine' in *The Politics of Truth and Reconciliation in South Africa* provides a rich discussion of the ways the statement taking was set up, and how English came to replace the original language version. The essays collected in Deborah Posel's and Graeme Simpson's (2002) *Commissioning the Past* pay attention to the language of the TRC, and the impact of language and terminology choices on its search for 'truth'. In his *Ambiguities of Witnessing: Law and Literature in the Time of the Truth Commission*, Mark Sanders (2007: 155) provides the most sustained reflection on the languages of the TRC:

> Repeated reference is made to the translation apparatus at the hearings, and to the policy of taking statements in the language chosen by the witness (*Truth Commission Report* 5:2-8, III; I:146-147, 298-299). The crucial fact that these statements were then 'record[ed] in English', (*Truth Commission Report* 5:5) is not, however, underlined. I will underline it: the fact that the report and the eleven million pages of transcripts are in English, and the original language less easily accessible on audio- and videotape housed at the National Archives of South Africa in Pretoria, means, once again, that the decolonising impulse to restoration and restitution is an equivocal one.

Sanders makes, in passing, the point that I want to develop more completely: that translation into English may at times not serve the best interests of those who are translated, nor of those who perform the labour.

Translation nowadays, in official contexts in South Africa, predominantly happens *into* English, out of other South African languages. The border crossings enrich English, the labour is performed by heteroglots for the benefit of monolingual English-speakers, who can thus 'afford' (to extend the economic metaphor) to remain monoglot since the work of heteroglossia and translating is performed by someone else. A further inequality of this situation is that many monolingual South Africans tend to be English-speakers, and tend to be the beneficiaries of racially and linguistically determined privileges. When translation takes place out of other South African languages into South African English, this monolingual privilege can be confirmed and extended. Here we see translation serving an agenda of neutralising accents and diluting heteroglossia.

Translation and lack of translation are themes running through many of the chapters in this book, most clearly in the chapter on the collaborative research project written up as *There was this Goat*, itself a reflection on translation, and on its value and its limitations. The discussion traces the many ways in which translation is used figuratively in *There was this Goat*; but also draws out the underlying tensions in the collaborative project. My own reading of *There was this Goat* seeks out moments where the project is questioned or where the collaborators are in conflict over the meaning of their work. Translation is best seen, I argue, as a site of conflict, rather than as a path to reconciliation and understanding.

In the chapter on teachers ('He places his chair against mine and translates') we read of teachers whose accented teaching practices make material understandable to their students. These HIV educators, who travel around the country with their mobile cinema, screen an autobiographical film in which their own vulnerability is very clearly to be seen. In their discussions with their audience (the viewers who come to see the film and to be educated) we see an excellent example of a teacher who speaks in the accent of his (they are all men) students. He is attuned to what he needs to know about them in order for them to learn. Another gifted teacher in the same chapter is the man we know as 'Sizwe' from Jonny Steinberg's (2009) book *Three Letter Plague*. Sizwe reveals himself to be a teacher who facilitates the learning of his pupil, Steinberg, but whose own relationship to language and to education is a darker theme in the book. The inequalities of access to education and to English skews what Steinberg and Sizwe can make of the knowledge shared between them.

A different approach to translation failure is that found in the chapter on early histories of translation in South Africa. Early colonial histories of South Africa contain many references to translators and interpreters, yet these linguistic transactions did not lead to situations of equality or mutuality (as those who use translation as a version of equality and learning about others may want to promise us). Instead, these early African translator figures were conscripted and viewed as agents of European mercantilism and colonial expansion. In this chapter we see most clearly the arguments against translation, as the discussion traces a continuing trend in the translational encounter in South Africa, where translation is done at the cost of African languages.

TOWARDS ACCENTEDNESS

I want this book to move beyond translation as a way of thinking about discourses of transformation, and instead develop the concept of accentedness. The term 'accent' is not used in this book in the strictly linguistic sense, not taken to be the auditory features of pronunciation which enable one to place the speaker socially and regionally (Crystal 1991: 2). The literature on accent is intent on differentiation and stratification, both of phonemes and of the ways in which we are placed and grouped in the world. The way in which it is used here is instead to denote the acknowledgement of a specific, even a 'local', orientation or field of reference; it is a figurative use of the term which is sometimes at odds with the ways in which the term is defined in linguistics. The way in which accent is used here is closer to that of Hamid Naficy in *An Accented Cinema: Exilic and Diasporic Filmmaking* (2001), but Naficy wants the concept to do very different work from the way I use it. For Naficy, accented discourse is a feature of displacement, a form of communication favoured by those whose work and lives are inflected by the experiences of diaspora and exile. In my work, the accent is, on the contrary, a way of thinking about 'home', and finding ways of reading and teaching that aim to understand and bring local meanings to bear on interpretation. My own use of the term also emphasises conflict and discord as features of accent, whereas Naficy's term is marked with diasporic longing and loss.

In the chapters that follow, accentedness is developed as a theoretical concept, through an examination of a range of texts, artworks, images and artefacts. Accent is, in the first place, understood as resistance to absorption. Njabulo Ndebele's challenge to the English Academy is a key text in this understanding of accentedness. I discuss Ndebele's work for a strand of ideas around accent, mother tongue and resistance to what he calls 'benign containment', framing the analysis of his work by an account of a staff seminar in which the seminar presenter, Tlhalo Raditlhalo, describes and performs not being understood. Instead of trying to show that Raditlhalo had in fact been 'understood', I argue that this resistance to being understood is what one needs to 'understand'; and discuss suspicion and mistrust as important components of accented discourse. Accentedness is thus not seen as a drive to reconciliation and homogeneity; instead it is an attitude that challenges and defies those in power and aims to bring to the surface conflictual histories.

In the third chapter, I analyse the work of artist and academic Thembinkosi Goniwe. An open letter to the South African National

Gallery, written as a young academic, provides a way of approaching Goniwe's project of resistance. I use Goniwe's theoretical work on representation to develop the concept of accentedness further, here focusing on language and the orientation of knowledge. Goniwe's work of art is interpreted as a visual form of accusation, forcing the viewer to adopt the position of someone who refuses to meet his gaze – even when one is doing precisely that. I discuss the performance of being misunderstood, and the insistence on misunderstanding, as a form of resistance and as a version of accentedness.

Another way of approaching resistance is theorised through the concept of address, understood in the first place as location (either from where something or someone comes or to where it goes), but also in the related sense of speaking or writing with a listener or reader in mind. In all the chapters of this book, intertextuality as a way towards interpreting a text is seen as potentially activist work. Making our thinking accented is a way of thinking about who we are addressing, and what they might know (and we ourselves might need to know). An important theoretical insight underpinning this argument is what Simon Gikandi calls 'reading the referent': to know which referent to invoke when reading a text. Gikandi reads a text by Dambudzo Marechera, including references to Shakespeare and also to Lobengula, the last king of the Matabele people. Gikandi shows that a particular reader will 'read over' Shakespeare (not finding it meaningful), and another over Lobengula, regarding either one or the other as not crucial to understanding the text. This does not mean the Shakespeare referent is unimportant. It does mean, though, that there is work to be done to inform oneself of the Lobengula reference, to become aware of the (linguistic, literary and historical) knowledge one might need to interpret a text – to 'read the referent' as Gikandi terms it.

In this way, then, address can be understood as a form of intertextuality and contextuality in action. Thinking about questions of address in the classroom, in these ways, can enhance teaching practice and influence the way students might learn. The related understandings of address also provide a way of imagining how words circulate among diverse audiences (a diversity of accents, diverse language backgrounds, and multiple contextual fields of reference). In this sense, too, the arguments aim at theorising a reading and teaching practice that places centrally the interrogation of a speaker's address (where we come from, where others come from, where the exchange is taking place).

This book is interested in two addresses, and here the word is used in its primary sense to understand where a reader is when she is reading (geographically, linguistically, imaginatively), and how that influences the way she reads. In debates around the changing role of the university in South Africa (and elsewhere, but the main interest of this work is in the South African case), there is a tension between various addresses. The debates over Africanisation, for example, can be understood as an attempt at bringing together the two (or more) addresses of each of our students, of developing a curriculum and teaching practice that can perform and effect coincidence between these addresses. The university is often a place that takes one away from 'home', but there are significant ways in which university learning and teaching can either acknowledge the diverse versions of the ordinary contextual fields of students, or unknowingly deny that these differences exist. The work I am describing aims to reverse, or at least draw attention to, this state of unknowingness. The activist work of creating accented thinking does not require, for example, that all South Africans know all the many (more than the eleven officially recognised) languages spoken in the country – although multilingualism is a clear advantage for the tradition the book advocates – but it is crucial to realise that there are things, and languages and contexts, that one does not know, and to acknowledge that one's own intertextual field is not the standard, one's own tastes not the norm.

In the discussion of Zoë Wicomb's body of work, the ideas of location and audience are theorised most clearly. Wicomb's work returns in various ways, creative and theoretical, to questions of home and homeliness. In this chapter the meanings of 'address' are investigated through a reading of a number of documents. One of these is a transcript of an unauthorised recording of an interview, in which Wicomb is under attack for not being 'at home', and for writing from an address different from that of the people she writes about. This unusual, overheard, conversation is read for what it reveals about audience and the location of the reader. A short story by Wicomb, 'The one that got away', is analysed alongside Wicomb's theoretical reflections on intertextuality and the particular meanings of South Africa in her work.

Wicomb's work is suspicious of origins and originals, and it is this theme that is developed in another way in the chapter on lost originals. Like many countries with violent histories of colonisation, South African life is marked by cultural and linguistic extinctions. It is the meaning of one such lost 'origin' that forms the topic of the chapter called 'The copy and the lost original' which traces the ways in which a particular set of documents and artefacts has entered academic and intellectual life: the documents now known as the Bleek-Lloyd archive. While the memorialisation of lost cultures and languages is no doubt commendable, this chapter shows that the academic and artistic pursuit of such a lost world risks placing the remembering as a new origin, thereby divesting us – the academics and intellectuals – of any complicity in the discovery and destruction.

ORDINARY READINGS

To return to a less theoretical understanding of the project, I end with a final set of ideas borrowed from Njabulo Ndebele: the ways in which we have come to understand what he has called, so influentially, 'ordinariness'. The argument I make wants to force us to consider the effect on our teaching of imagining a particular student's interpretations of a text as ordinary and not in need of remedial teaching. Many models of teaching in South Africa (as elsewhere) rely on patterns that borrow from missionary traditions; the one teacher reads from and illuminates the book to a learner who becomes increasingly worthy of the material. In this version of the teaching encounter, the student is the only one who needs to undergo transformation. Instead, what my book wants to investigate is the ways in which the teacher may need to learn, or an institution may need to be transformed. What is at issue here is to question the fact that what is 'ordinary' and normative is self-evident and natural to all. This way of understanding ordinariness unsettles and questions the dominance of English and of a misplaced trust in the disciplines (and our institutional locations) as unaccented, and without their own histories of implicit exclusion.

Ordinariness in this sense is not meant to refer merely to everydayness, but also to the location (or the address) of the ordinary. The imagined reader, rather than being understood as a reader who defines herself in terms of some accepted standard, is a reader who reads *at* her address, *from* her address, and in an accent that is informed by this location. While many would want to describe this imagined reader as a 'postcolonial subject', my argument wants to foreground the possible interpretations of a reader who has no interest in postcolonial theory. She is not a postcolonial subject in the sense that she has no knowledge of such a position. She is not a resistant reader, a reader talking or 'writing back' to a canon; she is just an ordinary reader – even the ideal reader for the way my project theorises reading. In time she may become a self-consciously postcolonial reader and theorist; but the argument does not require for her to enter into debate with this body of work.

In these final paragraphs I turn explicitly to teaching situations, and to an imagined provincial schoolgirl who may be able to enter an institution of higher learning. She is the reader I have had in my mind while writing this book. She is not necessarily the reader *for* the book itself, but for the way the book wants to theorise the reading practice and the relationship between teacher and student. She is an ordinary schoolgirl who has taken a book off a shelf in a poorly-resourced provincial library somewhere in South Africa. Or perhaps she has found it among other abandoned or given objects. The book she is beginning to read is not a book that has been written with her as a reader in mind (let's say the book is Charles Dickens's *Great Expectations*). Yet she is about to read and to make meaning of it for herself; she is about to read it in her own accent; an ordinary girl finding in it, and making for herself, what are, for her, ordinary meanings.

The implication of my argument in this book is that for those of us who are teachers, our work is to learn to read alongside her, to imagine sitting with her there where she is reading and to try to understand the meaning she makes. What we need is a teaching practice that can account for her engagement with the book as ordinary, in the sense of ordinary as accepted and normative. In the long ending of apartheid in South Africa, our work as scholars and teachers is to be attentive to readers like the one I have evoked, and to make the university not only a place that studies her, but where she can eventually come to study.

The first impetus behind the thinking in this book is that teaching, like learning, can be a form of activism, and that in our scholarship we can seek out texts, images and archives that are resistant to the enduring legacies of apartheid. In order to teach – and even to encounter in a university classroom – the girl I am thinking about, a teacher needs to learn to imagine and to respond to the contexts (the ordinary conditions) of her encounter with the book and with knowledge. It is an approach to teaching that requires an investment of work (the work of literacy, of girls' education as well as boys', of reversing ignorance, of learning other South African languages, of allowing oneself to show vulnerability), and this is the sense in which it is an activist practice. The understanding of this accented work is of something that is not simply there, self-evidently, but has to be *made* through our reading and teaching practice, and through the local intertextual fields we can learn to bring together. The argument here does not aim to create a tradition by seeking out unifying or national strands. Instead, it argues that difference and disagreement, rather than similarity and unity, are what distinguish this South African accent.

The arguments in this book thus seek out resistance, non-cooperation, performances and experiences of misunderstanding, as productive of, rather than as the opposite of, transformation.

The after-life of apartheid's lack of attention to this imagined accented reader is one of the challenges facing universities in South Africa, and a large literature and policy discourse have evolved to address exactly this. One thinks here of the work of Jonathan Jansen, Crain Soudien, Rachelle Kapp and Lucia Thesen as representative of the intellectual and practical research into the relationship between students and higher education institutions. My own book is not practical, nor does it provide policy outlines. But it is supportive of, and influenced by, this work. The argument made here is that as university teachers there are ways in which, through our scholarship and our teaching, we can make the university a place where the provincial schoolgirl's particular reading practice and its intertextual fields are accounted for and used.

Of course this does not mean that the meanings such a student finds and makes can replace other readings (that are differently intertextual), nor do I want to deny that the disciplines have particular languages and approaches that she, if she were to become a university student, will need to master. It does mean, though, that the burden of change is not only on this imagined girl reader, but on teachers and tertiary institutions too. We accept that the university is a place one comes to in order to be transformed (through knowledge, qualifications, experiences), to be made someone different from the person who entered through its doors. The university must feel enough 'like home' to someone like this girl reader (as far as her tastes, her experiences, her intertextual references are concerned), in order for her to begin her work of learning and changing. And this is the responsibility of us, her teachers, and the purpose of our scholarship – to build the university.

The schoolgirl reader I invoked is someone I hope at some stage to encounter in a university classroom, and my work in this book is to think of how I can become the kind of teacher she needs and deserves. In this book I aim to develop a theory that can account for her reading practices, and not assume that what she brings to the text (or it to her) is in need of remedial work. Of course, in the academy she can and should acquire the skills that will make her able to generate other readings – readings that will draw on the traditions of the university and the historically deter-mined practices of the disciplines – but as her teacher I need to imagine and theorise her primary, accented reading; and in my teaching practice I must be able to account for her and for it. There are of course grammars and vocabularies that are at home in the disciplines. The argument insists, though, that the disciplines have an obligation to theorise and to acknowledge their responsibility to these other readings, the readings that are generated in her contextual setting. The disciplines, in this version of the encounter, need to include her address (where she is when she is reading 'at home') in the way they imagine themselves and the scenes of their production and transmission. And related to this is a reflection on the purposes and aims of our scholarship, to whose benefit we research and study and teach, and how we imagine the scholar of the future.

The book's argument has grown out of my own teaching and research practices, in classrooms in South Africa and in London; and in response to thinking about what my particular accent (both in the meaning of my South-African inflected speech as well as my particular interest in developing accented points of view) means in the classroom. One theme that has run through many of the teaching situations that inform this book is a reflection on the languages of the teaching encounter itself, and the language histories present in the classroom. In South African classrooms, I found myself in front of groups of students with diverse and complex language biographies, and in the classroom we spoke (mostly) in English. But the English of the classroom was skewed by the fact that in the same classroom there were students who had always, and always only, used English to think and write and read. In classrooms in the UK (at the School of Oriental and African Studies in London), it turned out that only some members of the class were first-language speakers of English, and most of the students in the class were studying an African language as part of their degrees. In this surprising sense, the 'accent' in the classroom in the United Kingdom was stronger than in many classrooms in which I had taught in South Africa, where it was possible to study at a university without any knowledge of a (South) African language other than English, and where it was just possible to imagine that monolingualism was the norm.

The challenge in the South African classroom was to maintain an awareness of the fact that the classroom (in an 'English' department) required of some to translate their words and thoughts into 'English'. Of course all of these students could speak 'English', as first, or sometimes fourth or fifth languages. But my argument is interested in asymmetrical language situations in multilingual classrooms, where some students in the group speak only one language – which happens to be the language in which all discussion takes place. Of course there were students like this in the classroom in London too, but the institution where these students were learning assumed that learning African languages was to be encouraged and in some cases a requirement of a degree course. In a classroom where this is not the case, the role and status of the seemingly neutral language (and those who speak only this one language) needs to be a topic of discussion. In other words, in classrooms we need to create a sense of English as a language in which one can develop and express accented ways of thinking; and we need to face up to the inequalities inherent in teaching and learning in English. In addition to this is the fact that the pursuit of multilingualism is a crucial aspect of this activist work of intertextuality. The multilingual and accented classroom is the ideal classroom, or rather such a classroom is utterly ordinary (rather than a difficult or challenging exception).

The way in which this argument developed was through thinking about accented versions of 'English' in the classroom. In the first place, even before the language enters the disciplines, it means that each student in a class could expect to hear her or his name pronounced in a way that was close to the way she or he would say and hear it 'at home'. In South Africa, the histories of naming and renaming are multiple and revealing, often to the point where African names were declared (by teachers, priests or employers) as 'impossible' to pronounce. In South African classrooms, it is an expected moment, the moment when one has to ask of a student whether their name has been pronounced correctly. Surprising, and illuminating, to me was that this was a challenge I faced again in the classroom in London, where many students had names that were for example Swedish or Finnish, or in one case an Anglicised Zulu surname that I pronounced, incorrectly to *his* ear, with a South African (in this case meaning Zulu) accent. In the context of this classroom, what to me seemed like the correct pronunciation (a Zulu surname pronounced using Zulu phonemes) was not the correct one, proving that intertextuality is unpredictable and contextual. In this classroom my South African accent was, in this case, not the appropriate one.

My formulation of learning to read in a South African accent can be understood as a form of activist and resistant labour. It is the work that needs to be done towards developing a reading and teaching practice which will inform itself of other accents and addresses, and which will develop sensitivity to multiple locations, intertexts and registers. This inevitably means that the present study is drawn to texts and images that are self-consciously interested in questions of divided audiences, and that attempt to translate themselves (or resist translation), and to texts that thematise accent, intertextuality or disagreement. The argument in this book builds up a picture of what 'South African accented' thinking might look and sound like: a point of view that is at home in a non-monolingual voice (even if it happens to be written in one language only), that shows an awareness of multiple scenes of reception, and shows evidence of having imagined an audience beyond the self-same.

How to read, how to teach, how to listen: these are the questions addressed in this book – and how this is transformative work, making us the kind of teachers that can teach the students we will have, and for these students in turn to become the future citizens, scholars and academics we need. It is not a book that is interested, in the first place, in how the university can make students into something and someone else, but instead it is interested in how the university and teaching machine can respond, and through this response perform the activist work of *becoming* a South African accented place of learning.

One might think that teaching and reading in a South African accent is a natural thing for South Africans to do; but this book argues that it is a critical and reading position that will require ongoing and continuous work, and also that it is a position that can be adopted anywhere. In this way it is not an essentialist position, and nor is it even synonymous with speaking in a South African accent; it is perfectly possible to speak using South African accented English (or rather one of the many versions of such an accent) without adopting this position. In this sense my argument is non-nativist, and does not assume that anyone simply 'has' this accented point of view. The argument is not made at the level of language, although a classroom where every student speaks (or is learning) more than one language would go some way to creating the right conditions for accented thought. Language facility alone is not a test either (one can think here of many ways of learning and speaking a language that do not aim at imagining the position of the addressee, but instead aim to maintain and perpetuate power).

The location of the speaker and the reader I imagine through this work – the address, if you like – is one that does not exclude teachers and readers of South African material in, say, Nairobi or Istanbul. The approach taken in this book is one that is deeply interested in who performs the labour of making a new South African order, and also in who will get to benefit from this new order. In my version of this labour, the main burden of the work will fall on monolingual South Africans (English-speaking and Afrikaans-speaking), who tend to be the inheritors of white privilege. As the argument will show, this activism can be performed anywhere, and is not limited by region or location. In this sense it is an attitude which can be developed wherever there is the will to do so. The work of this book is intended to theorise and to document instances of accented thinking and writing, and the creation of new archives that will allow us to write our fractured histories and understand the conflicted present.

Chapter 2

THERE WAS THIS MISSING
QUOTATION MARK

ONE way of talking about the South African Truth and Reconciliation Commission (TRC) has been to use the language of learning and teaching. Those who delivered their testimonies were sometimes described as the teachers, or the Commission itself was described as a teaching machine; those who listened were the learners. In this understanding of testimony, listening and learning ideally bring about a transformation in the listener. The transformation, in turn, will lead to nation building through this collective exercise of learning and teaching. The book *There was this Goat: Investigating the Truth Commission Testimony of Notrose Nobomvu Konile* was published in 2009. In *There was this Goat*, we read an account of testimony as pedagogy, as formulated by Shoshana Felman and Dori Laub in their influential book *Testimony: Crises of Witnessing in Literature, Psychoanalysis, and History*:

> ... the task of testimony is to impart ... knowledge: a first-hand, car-
> nal knowledge of victimisation, of what it means to be 'from here'... a
> first-hand knowledge of a historical passage through death, and of the

way life will forever be inhabited by that passage and by that death; knowledge of the way in which 'this history concerns us all' (quoted in Krog, Mpolweni and Ratele 2009: 26).

This chapter explores who the beneficiaries are of teaching and learning: in the first place the learning and teaching of the TRC that is the subject of *There was this Goat*; but also the learning and teaching involved in the research project that became the book *There was this Goat*, a multilingual and multidisciplinary research project based at a South African University, the University of the Western Cape. The project has an autoethnographic component: we read not only the findings of the report but also the researchers' individual and collective reflections on the nature of the knowledge contained in it. Discussing the book in this chapter, I highlight one theme in particular: who is to benefit from learning. In the case of the research project that means thinking about who will benefit from reading and from writing the book; and who will benefit from what listeners and readers can learn from the testimony of Mrs Konile.

The beginnings of the research project are described for the reader of *There was this Goat*, between two sets of three tildes (~). The choice of the tilde as the division between sections might be neutral, but one possible meaning of the symbol is 'approximately': in other words, similar but not quite the same. In lexicography it can refer to deleted or omitted words; and in phonetics it is used as a pronunciation indicator. All these meanings are relevant in a book so interested in the deleted voice and the limits of transcription and translation. So here the three tildes can be a reminder of all that has been omitted or cannot be transcribed:

> When Antjie was appointed at the University of the Western Cape (UWC), she asked Nosisi Mpolweni, from the Xhosa Department, and Kopano Ratele, from the Psychology Department and Women and Gender Studies, to join her in a reading of Mrs Konile's testimony. She presented the possible conversation between two white people ... to explain the problems that Mrs Konile's testimony poses for people brought up and educated within a racist system and ideology. Nosisi and Kopano became interested in Mrs Konile's testimony and soon the three met weekly around the testimony, becoming a team with its own constantly changing dynamics and progress.
>
> From this point onwards, the journey will be made mostly by 'we'. At times the three of us would make contributions as individuals, but

the bulk of this book was built up over two years of weekly conversations, readings, discussions, writing together, presenting and talking
(Krog, Mpolweni and Ratele 2009: 40).

Elsewhere we read about how the multidisciplinary, multilingual research
group saw their work: 'Bit by bit we learned how better to "hear" one
another from different cultures and personal backgrounds. We talked,
read, listened, disagreed and journeyed together. We were not there yet,
but something important was happening. We found, unexpectedly, that
our working method became not only learning but a source of enrichment
and friendship' (Krog, Mpolweni and Ratele 2009: 43). The benefits of
the research project to Mrs Konile are a topic that recurs in the book. The
project is based at a research and teaching institution which, we read,
'reaffirmed its commitment to ethical research'. The researchers had to
fill in a variety of forms in which they agreed to 'inform Mrs Konile of
[their] full intentions and the outcome of [the] project, as well as not to
pay her for her information' (Krog, Mpolweni and Ratele 2009: 125).
In this 'ethical' understanding of the research project, the gain is all on
the side of those who have signed the form – the form that ensures all
research is 'ethical'. The three researchers decide that the human thing
to do, in this case, is not the same as the ethical thing as defined by the
forms they have signed. They give Mrs Konile gifts to thank her for her
time, and for the narrative she has to recount again. In this way, the gain
of the project exceeds, and also brings into question, what the academic
ethical code can imagine.

The scene on the cover of the book shows a group of goats outside
the wooden door of a house, and the same photograph appears inside
the book, where the caption reads: 'Goats form an integral part of life
(physical and spiritual) and are everywhere in Indwe. Here three of them
rest at a front door.' This is not necessarily the house of Mrs Konile,
although it is in her village; below is another photograph, which *is* of her
house (there are also some photographs of the inside of the house – and
the discussion below returns to these photographs and their place in the
project). The researchers had considered putting a portrait of Mrs Konile
on the cover. Instead, they have chosen a portrait of some goats, echoing
the deliberately opaque title.

It is worth considering the difference it would make to have had Mrs
Konile's portrait on the cover. The goats are the referent in the testimony
of Mrs Konile, a referent that seemed not to make sense in the transcript.
Choosing the goats, what the project uses as its icon is *incomprehensibility*,

or the need to examine incomprehensibility. By putting on the cover the photograph of Mrs Konile, one might argue, there would have been a false supposition of her ownership of the project, that the project could ventriloquise her words. Instead the cover, as well as the title, draws attention exactly to the gap between Mrs Konile's words and the research project's questions and ethical constraints. The project cannot restore her words to fullness, nor give her any restitution. In this sense, the gain to her of retelling her story is small, and the researchers are aware of this and try to reflect on the implications of it. In an early section of the book Krog writes (2009: 19):

> It is said that we *tell* stories so that we do not die of truth. But we also tell stories to know who we are and to make sense of the world. We constitute our social identities through narrative and, although life is much more than stories, stories also try to create an order in the chaos of our lives. Stories in their widest sense can be used to bring order, or tell about chaos.
>
> We *listen* to one another's stories so that we share carrying the truth. But we also listen to stories in order to become, for one brief moment, somebody else, to be somewhere we've not been before. We listen to stories in order to be changed. And at the end of the story we do not want to be the same person as the one who started listening.

Krog shows how this ideal of listening and learning is adopted by the three researchers, who start to listen to one another, and through learning to listen also learn to tell ('tell stories to know who we are') differently. The description of the project ends with two scenes of disappointment. One of these is to do with the awkward way in which the three researchers respond to the shared knowledge that Mrs Konile has died during the writing of the book. The other is to do with the final conversation between the researchers, a conversation about the limits of the project and the limits of the 'shared' nature of becoming someone different – but first it is worth summarising what this really wonderful project does achieve. The book provides a skilful and many-layered investigation and restoration of the testimony of Mrs Konile to the TRC human rights violations hearings in April 1996. In one reading, it is an excellent example of the difference a respectful translation can make to the 'original' words of a speaker, especially one who is not a powerful person. The text uses words such as 'excavation' and 'opening up' about its desires and aims, clearly pointing the way to a reading that leads to 'greater understanding'. It starts out as an investigation (an uncovering, an opening up) of the influence of cultural codes and filters on the way we understand one another (2009: 122), and can therefore be read as part of a nation building project. In this reading, the book's aims are in accordance with some ways of understanding the TRC as a process that means to uncover the past and, through that, point the way to a future of openness and reconciliation.

The text of *There was this Goat* develops a vision of a 'nuanced South Africanness' (2009: 102), a South Africanness that is aware of difference, and which acknowledges the need for labour to be performed that will 'excavate' and 'open up' discourses and utterances that are not immediately understood by all. This is the way the book wants to be read, but – perhaps not surprisingly in a co-authored project where the authors themselves seem at times to be *performing* code differences and disagreements – there is at least one other strong trend in the book, one that runs exactly counter to 'understanding' and reconciliation. In this reading, the project has as one of its aims precisely the insistence on a *lack* of understanding, and on a level of mistrust about how and to whose benefit 'understanding' is to be achieved. I present the reconciliatory way of reading the book as the first reading, and the project is analysed for what it can reveal about the ways in which it is possible to excavate and unearth Mrs Konile's original meaning, embedded in its own indigenous codes. I accept and use the following terms: original, embedded, own, indigenous. My argument then moves on to the other, more resistant, way of reading the text, in which I develop a reading which questions the assumptions and terms of the previous section and ask: why might one *not* want every reader or listener to 'understand', and in particular why might one not want Mrs Konile to be the one performing the labour that will lead to a mutual 'understanding'.

My argument seeks out moments in the text where non-understanding and mis-understanding are presented as the very aim of the text (or rather of this complex collection of texts). In this reading, a related set of ideas is traced: that of the location of the attempt to understand (the 'address' of the reading), and the nature of the reported speech – the 'missing quotation mark' (2009: 94) as one of the researchers terms it. Put differently, this part of the argument is interested in how Mrs Konile's reported speech runs the risk of being absorbed into another speech with another set of codes and desires, those of the text quoting and containing the reported speech. These two sets of ideas relate to the insistence on precisely *not understanding*. There are, we see in the text, many ways of *not understanding*. The address of the reading (where, by whom, for whose benefit) affects the ability and desire to either understand or to resist understanding.

There was this Goat: Investigating the Truth Commission Testimony of Notrose Nobomvu Konile is co-authored by three academics/writers: Antjie Krog, Nosisi Mpolweni and Kopano Ratele, and copyright in this text is held by them collectively. On the title page of the text their names appear visually linked as 'Antjie Krog ~ Nosisi Mpolweni ~ Kopano Ratele', further emphasising the collaborative nature of the project.

> This final manuscript arose out of four kinds of texts: original primary texts of testimony gathered by the Truth Commission and also by ourselves; texts we wrote personally by ourselves focusing on something particular in our different fields; texts written physically together in the office, with everybody talking and formulating, and with either Kopano or Antjie typing; and, finally, texts made up from recorded and transcribed discussions/interviews/conversations/opinions/e-mails (2009: 45).

This paragraph draws attention to the collection of texts as evidence of the layeredness of the research, and thus the density of attention and elucidation. The description also makes us aware of the collaborative nature of the research, the fact that the work does not only aim to create reconciliation and unity but it also *performs* it explicitly. In the paragraph just before this, we read: 'And Mrs Konile was a constant presence. She was, in a way, as much an author of the manuscript as any of us' (2009: 45). So the name of a fourth co-author (the person who is the author of the unifying original text) appears on the book's cover: Notrose Nobomvu Konile. But she is moved out of the list of authors' names and into the title of the book. The first part of the title ('*There was this Goat*') is a quotation from her testimony, and on the cover it is written in cursive script as if in handwriting, to show that these are her actual words.

Mrs Konile, if she is to be seen as a co-author of the book, is clearly a different kind of author to the others. Whereas the location (the address if one likes) of their work is the university and the publisher, her address is her rural home. Her words appear always in reported and transcribed form, unlike those of the other three, who comment on her words and on their own responses. Mrs Konile's words thus appear in quotation marks (originally in the official version, the TRC report, 'misquoted') as the text to which the other texts respond. One of the researchers in particular,

Nosisi Mpolweni, sets herself the task of restoring Mrs Konile's words, and during a visit to Mrs Konile's home Mrs Konile repeats (and adds more information to) the original narrative. While she is not on the cover, her home town, Indwe, is, and photographs of her and her home appear in the chapter about the visit by the researchers. We read that the discovery of the word 'Indwe' in the testimony is a key to placing Mrs Konile's narrative and her accent. Her location (her 'address') thus leads to the uncovering of the lost meanings of her 'original' words.

The book is dedicated to 'Mrs Notrose Nobomvu Konile and her family', turning the 'address' of the book back to Mrs Konile, placing the reader next to her. The dedication is intended to acknowledge Mrs Konile's assistance and generosity, and 'repay' her (a concern especially in the chapter about the visit). The reader is not directly addressed by the dedication, but we overhear it, as if it is meant, at least partly, as a performance to be overheard. Thus the address of the book is 'return to sender', and the reader is left to imagine what kind of gift this text might be to Mrs Konile. As it turns out, Mrs Konile dies before the book is finalised, adding another layer of poignancy to the overheard dedication.

In one of the photographs, a younger lively-looking Mrs Konile faces the camera, seemingly addressing the photographer. Mrs Konile is, as the caption informs us, wearing 'traditional amaXhosa attire consisting of ochre/red cloth braided with black, worn with beads and a decorated *kopdoek* (headscarf) stylishly folded. This photograph was taken at a wedding and was kindly supplied by Thandeka Konile.'

In another photograph an older Mrs Konile is seated in her home with two of the researchers, Kopano Ratele and Nosisi Mpolweni. The third, Antjie Krog, takes the photograph, and so is present in the room but is not visible. Strangely, Mrs Konile appears cropped half out of the picture, visually distanced from the other two by the background – behind her a brick wall, behind them a painted section of wall. Mrs Konile sits with part of her face visible, while two of the researchers look at her, Kopano Ratele is pointing a small camera at her, a video recorder camera on a tripod is facing her, and on the table we see a microphone and a tape recording device capturing her speech. Mrs Konile, multiply recorded and documented, is, however, almost invisible in the photograph; instead what is recorded very clearly is the *process* of recording and documenting the visit.

The photograph is taken using yet another recording device by the third member of the research team, who is in this frame recording the record-ing, transcribing the transcription of the event of meeting Mrs Konile in

Mrs Konile in her home (seated right) visited by the three researchers,
Kopano Ratele (left) and Nosisi Mpolweni (centre). The third researcher Antjie
Krog is taking the photograph.

her own home. The text shows that the third researcher's lack of facility
in Xhosa means that this conversation is inaccessible to her, and so she
wanders around the home taking photographs. The photograph can thus
be read also as a document of the three researchers' relationship to the
research, and to Mrs Konile's speech. The visual absence of Antjie Krog
from the photograph, the absence of the non-Xhosa speaking member of
the group, records also her uncomprehending absence from the conversation, an absence which is reflected again in the written transcript. Here is
the first and most clearly visible form of *not understanding* in the project:
not understanding the exchange taking place in Xhosa. The fact that we
read the transcript in English means of course that the reader is imagined
precisely not in the room, not next to Mrs Konile, but is outside the

room, outside the Xhosa language conversation. Someone has translated the text for us; someone has performed this labour to let us into the room (but watching, not taking part).

The analysis I offer of this photograph is not meant to imply that I think the researchers are unaware of these multiple levels of recording, transcription and exclusion; on the contrary, my reading of the photograph is very much in line with their own understanding of their project. In this book, which is itself a transcript of a collaborative research project, the researchers return to the invisibility and unreadability of Mrs Konile and her words, revisiting their understandings of the testimony, and their understandings of their and others' (non)-understandings. In the very first references to Mrs Konile, in the book's Introduction, we read that in the TRC transcript she is presented without a first name, and that she 'looks as if she could disappear at any moment', even at times 'holding a big white handkerchief over much of her face' (2009: 1) almost as if she is willing herself to be invisible. Resistance to being understood is a theme that runs through the book, complicating and questioning 'understanding'. The resistance to being understood and to being understand*ing* of others also has a clear echo in Mrs Konile's resistance to forgiving the killers of her son – an unwillingness that distinguished her from the mothers of the other sons killed in the same attack. One thinks here too of examples from the history of the TRC, where families refused to go along with it, the most famous case probably that of the Biko family, who refused to take part in the hearings (Nkosinathi Biko 2000: 193).

On a practical level, the text of *There was this Goat* is an analysis of a transcript – the transcript of Mrs Konile's testimony to the TRC, included here in the Xhosa text as well as in the 'original' English translation, a translation that turns out not to be a true reflection of her words and meaning. The first version of this transcript that the reader reads is that called the 'official' testimony as found on the Truth Commission website (2009: 12) but we read in *There was this Goat* that there was no trace of her name in the index and under the heading of the Gugulethu Seven incident, her surname was given incorrectly as 'Khonele'. Mrs Konile's real name is Notrose Nobomvu Konile, but even in her identity document, as she pointed out many years later, her second name was given incorrectly as Nobovu' (2009: 4). We are provided with instances of the lack of respect shown to Mrs Konile, a lack of respect that this collaborative research project wishes to reverse. There follows the rationale for the project and the book:

'So what?' you might well ask. Why is it important to try to understand this unmentioned, incorrectly ID-ed, misspelt, incoherently testifying, translated and carelessly transcribed woman? In the pages that follow, we have tried to give our reasons (2009: 4).

And later on in the book we read about the group's working method:

Our working method was as important as what we found. We first discussed the official version of Mrs Konile's testimony on the Truth and Reconciliation Commission website, and all three of us found it largely incoherent and incomprehensible. Among the possible explanations was faulty translation or an unintelligible witness, which in turn opened up another set of questions. Was Mrs Konile unintelligible because she was traumatised or because she simply did not understand what had happened and what was happening around her? We ordered the cassette with the original Xhosa version from the South African National Archives and used our different disciplines, backgrounds, cultures and languages to gradually devise a way to 'hear' Mrs Konile.

The working method was, first, to transcribe the Xhosa language testimony, then to retranslate this into English, thus offering a different version to the official translation:

It soon became evident that incomprehension had been created at different stages of the process towards an official version. There were ordinary interpretation mistakes and transcription mistakes, as well as a third category that we called 'cultural untransferables' – in other words, cultural codes and references that did not survive the interpretation process. The process we engaged in was rather like an archaeological excavation – every weekly session unearthed a new reality closer and closer to a multifaceted and complex original (2009: 44-5).

This transcript is re-translated and re-interpreted from a set of tapes of Mrs Konile, making the audio recording the more original. The text contains the original transcript, which is revealed to be a poor transcript. It also contains an improved transcript, with notes as to the conception and development of the new, improved transcript, a truer 'original'. Reference is made to the theoretical issues surrounding transcription and simultaneous translation, and we then find a transcript of a conversation between translators and interpreters. In addition, we read the researchers' comments on the project in transcripts of various conversations between them. All of these meanings of transcript problematise the notion of dialogue being *the same* as the transcript of that same dialogue, and show an awareness of the intimate and often vexed relationship between speaker and transcriber, speaker and translator.

The project could be seen as an attempt at restoring Mrs Konile's identity and speech, to provide her and her words with a better, more informed, more suitably coded interpretation. The text suggests that if Mrs Konile were to be listened to, and decoded, using her 'indigenous framework', her speech would be restored to its original fullness. It is this assumption of sameness and fullness, this belief in homogeneity and origins, which is resisted at other instances in the text. These resistant moments are most often attached to the signature of Kopano Ratele, and I return to them later.

There is another aspect of this text that raises, again, the issue of learning and teaching and the benefits of knowledge transmission. There occur in the text clusters of words that draw attention to testimony and transcription as akin to, a version of, the relationship between teacher and student. The location of the research project is, we know already, the University of the Western Cape. The location for the conversations between the three authors, we read, is originally an office at this university, and the final meetings are again held in this office. Thus we are led to think about the location of knowledge production, and the ways in which education can transform learners (and teachers).

Parts of the text want to understand the TRC testimonies as a form of education, and this of course raises questions my own work asks. To whose benefit is this teaching, who is teaching and who is learning, and what kind of transformation is effected by the learning?

> By presenting our research in seminars, conferences and journals, were we not making too strong a link between witnessing and peda-gogy? Did we believe that listening to trauma might lead to a true en-counter with another and a cross-cultural engagement with The Other in a way that would resituate history in our understanding, instead of eliminating it? (2009: 124).

Taking, for the moment, this insight that what was said at the hearings of the TRC is like an education, it is worth looking at the versions of this education the text develops. Each of the authors has a distinctive voice or accent, and each adopts a set of positions with regard to translation and interpretation (in the more and the less technical versions of the word), as well as to questions of learning and teaching. Through presenting the position of each of the three co-authors, the next section shows how questions of containment and pedagogy are linked in this text. The version of the encounter associated with Nosisi Mpolweni ('I, [*Nosisi*]') perhaps raises the fewest questions. In a sense the text is produced by her, she is the one who re-translates and re-transcribes Mrs Konile's words from the tapes. She is also the one who seems to hold the key to placing and decoding Mrs Konile's words (her accent, her references, her geographical placement), and acts as guide into Mrs Konile's world for the other researchers, and for the readers of the completed text. She is the ideal translator-interpreter, someone whose facility is so well-matched that it risks making itself invisible. The narrative of her work, what she allows others to 'learn' from it, is a narrative of the ideal teacher, teaching us how to read, and teaching us in particular how to read Mrs Konile's words.

The text introduces her in the following way:

> Nosisi was the first to put in long solid hours transcribing and trans-lating. Working right there at the edge where the text was starting to open up, she was the first to identify decisive elements for our re-search. Nosisi also played an important role in determining and eas-ing our interaction with the Konile family and their original context.

Nosisi Mpolweni's work is the work of making Mrs Konile's words sensible, audible and intelligible. She does this through drawing on her historical relationship with women who are 'like' Mrs Konile, and her knowledge of the kind of relationship she might have with someone who is like Mrs Konile. Her text wants to be a relative to Mrs Konile's, her words want to have a kinship relation to the words of the testimony and, subsequently, the words of Mrs Konile when the researchers meet her in person. She is the one who restores the missing quotation mark by trying to reconstitute what Mrs Konile understands by her words and not being overly interested in how she can make others understand. This, then, is one way of thinking of a translator: someone who is able to imagine being a relative to the author, someone whose text is kin (akin) to the original text. She is able to be the guide, to be the one who opens up the text, because she can imagine being close to Mrs Konile. Mpolweni writes:

The discovery of the word 'Indwe' was a revelation. It swung the whole testimony from the realm of the incomprehensible to the comprehensible, and was the single biggest contributor to making the testimony coherent. It is an example of how a transcription mistake in the English version could be detected through pronunciation peculiarities in the original sound text (2009: 50).

Nosisi Mpolweni is able to understand the accent of Mrs Konile, and this accent places the text and the speaker geographically, socially and linguistically. The translation does not try to find equivalences in another code, but wants to stay as close to the text as it can. She is not only thinking about the text as a translator would, that is, thinking in the first place of how to give access to those who do not understand the text. She is also restoring the text to itself, paying it respect and attention for its own sake. This is an important point, which will be contrasted later to other ways of seeing the testimony, ways that are more interested in the testimony as something which needs to be opened up so that it can be translated for an audience who is *not* like Mrs Konile.

In the chapter that recounts the visit to Mrs Konile, the first few pages of transcription deal with placing people socially and within their kinship relations and geographical locations. Nosisi Mpolweni asks Mrs Konile to repeat her family's genealogy, and Mrs Konile inserts a series of phrases with the intention of placing her, locating her. ('That's it! I have finished now. I come from the eMaGqwashwini clan'; 'Yes, that is our origin.') In the conversation, Mrs Konile addresses Mpolweni as 'Mama' even though she herself is older, later as Sisi and 'my child' and once even as 'Nono', a term of endearment typically reserved for children:

> During the interview, I held back the Nosisi in me, I noticed that I was behaving as if I was Mrs Konile's daughter. It facilitated a particular kind of interaction and I think she spoke more easily to me. The mother-daughter relationship is safer… She asked our clan names and that sort of established that we are all family. This tracing of genealogy created a wonderful equality and sameness among us (2009: 137).

Mpolweni's part of the text reveals a continued reflection on its relationship to Mrs Konile. In a statement that the text does not develop or explain, we read of Mpolweni saying to the other researchers that they have to think about 'survival' again – one could take it to refer also to the translation project, to attention to that which survives, what remains behind in a translation and in the translation process. In this understanding of the translation process, great care is taken not to insert the words into a context that renders them invisible and empties them of meaning. The sections of the text that Mpolweni writes show hardly any interest in questions of audience (crucial in translation studies), or in who might be listening. She is not particularly interested in the dissemination of the words; her concern is with her words being like a daughter (respectful, loving, faithful, rooted) to the words of Mrs Konile. Her labour is not primarily performed to let others in, to translate Mrs Konile's words out of their own context into a context where they are readily understandable, nor to communicate understanding of those who do not understand.

The two other authors, Krog and Ratele, each develop their own version of engagement with the aims of the research project, a project which centres on questions of translation and how this relates to learning and understanding. In the Krog sections, the question that recurs is how can she, Krog, be taught by Mrs Konile and, in turn, how can she teach Mrs Konile that not all Boers have the same face. In this understanding of the TRC, and of dialogue and translation, there is a desire to impart knowledge – the kind of knowledge that leads to change. Krog's theory of translation is one that seeks to effect transformation in the receiver of the translated text, to become someone other through understanding and inhabiting the words of someone else.

In the text associated with Kopano Ratele, on the other hand, there is an insistence on the limits to 'understanding'. Ratele insists on what he calls learning to 'experience the gap', the gap between the untranslated and translated versions of experiences and texts. He also wants what Mrs Konile has to teach not to be to the benefit of whites. In other words, the labour involved in making Mrs Konile understood is not intended to benefit those who feel themselves to be loyal to 'white' concerns. Like Mpolweni, he is not overly concerned about whether the translation opens up the words to white listeners. But what his work *is* deeply interested in is the distorting effect of this imagined, spectral eavesdropping white ear.

The research questions of *There was this Goat* can be read as a development of some of the issues Krog had already written about in her trilogy *Country of my Skull*, *A Change of Tongue* and *Begging to be Black*. In this work, she had evolved her theory of translation as a way of becoming someone other, of inhabiting the position of the other (text or person); the links between this model and the work of the TRC and nation building are illuminating and fruitful. In this present book,

Krog wants Mrs Konile to be changed (to be changed by seeing Krog as a person despite the fact that she is white, despite the fact that she does not 'understand' Mrs Konile's words), and she also hopes to change the opinion of some readers, to make them see the worth of trying to 'understand' Mrs Konile. The text wants us to pay attention to the 'address' of a text (Mrs Konile's words), and so it is worth trying to do the same for *There was this Goat*.

The conversations start with the other two invited researchers (Mpolweni the translation specialist, Ratele the psychologist) reading a staged and fictional conversation between two people, what Krog calls a 'possible white conversation'. We read as if we are overhearing this imagined conversation which is private, as if it was not meant to be transcribed. The imagined conversation lets us listen to two people 'brought up and educated within a racist system and ideology' (2009: 40) discuss the ways in which they cannot understand Mrs Konile. Krog telephones a cousin to verify some of the racist views she includes in her imagined dialogue. The dialogue is written in English (and there are no notes in the volume to indicate that her sections of the book started their life in Afrikaans as some of her other books have done). But the language implied in the dialogue is 'white language'. The whiteness of the dialogue inheres in the value system of the speakers, and in their imagined inability to 'understand' those who are imagined to be different from them.

So Krog creates, imagines, a dialogue in which her white interlocutors express a lack of understanding of Mrs Konile. This incomprehensibility is of course what the whole research project is about, but I want to distinguish between different ways of 'not understanding'. The 'not understanding' Krog stages is one that presumes that there are differences between the speakers (two whites) and those they are speaking about (black South Africans).

There are other moments in Krog's work where she gives voice to the kinds of opinions expressed in the white conversation. One assumes she does not share these views; yet her motivation for including them is opaque. Is she performing a certain kind of Afrikaner (or 'Boer' as this text often terms it) identity, in order to distinguish herself from it? Her invocation of her cousins and brothers, to speak about white prejudice and racism, often marks the moments in her text that alienate me as a reader. I am drawn to much in the project of 'Krog', but want not to associate with the voices she seems so eager to put in quotation marks, to include in her writing. Yet in this imagined possible conversation, she is giving voice to 'white' opinions in a text that is exactly not trying to pay attention to such opinions, and one has to wonder why. One obvious explanation is that many white people do hold those opinions. But there is another, more complex, possibility. Krog is holding up these voices, this conversation, as a way of showing (herself and her reader, and Mrs Konile) that she is not like that, not like them. She wants Mrs Konile to be understood, and the project is partly aimed at the speakers in the 'white conversation', to try to make them 'understand' Mrs Konile. But also, significantly, to make Mrs Konile understand her, Krog.

What seems clear is that an imagined white audience remains a central concern in Krog's work – even when this audience is held up as something she wants to move away from. Perhaps it is too much to ask of a researcher to imagine a conversation in which her own presence is an irrelevance; but Krog's interest in her white readers does sometimes anger her co-researcher Ratele. When Krog wishes Mrs Konile to see a different kind of Boer face, she is still providing a quotation mark to these other voices, these other 'possible white conversations'; she is allowing them into the text and giving prominence and visibility to this kind of *not understanding*.

Read another way, the text could say that Krog performs a kind of voice, the untransformed white voice, in order to exercise how far she herself has been transformed. In her final not-saying goodbye to Mrs Konile, this is her regret – that she did not have the opportunity to perform a new kind of whiteness, a new kind of Afrikaner face. There is here a belief in the existence of such a thing as an Afrikaner face. In her introduction to the reissued edition of David Goldblatt's photographic essay on Afrikaners, *Some Afrikaners Revisited*, she writes (2007: 29), in response to the question of whether Afrikaners look different from other people:

> It is something here, between the nose and the mouth. Perhaps more towards the eyes … Man can be assimilated by a country. There is an x and a y in the air and in the soil of a country, which slowly permeate and assimilate him to the type of aboriginal inhabitant, even to the point of slightly remodelling his physical features. The foreign country somehow gets under the skin of those born in it.

In order to have a theory of the transformed Afrikaner, one must have a concept of an untransformed (original) Afrikaner, an assumption that such a person in fact exists. Her understanding of transformation assumes the existence of a deep structure. This is in many ways a very appealing idea, offering the possibility of change and transformation. But it is an idea that places the 'white conversation' as the origin, the source; and, significantly, assumes that there is such a thing as 'white' and 'black' in the first place. Her transformational grammar of identity relies on the fact that the deep structure is racialised, and that this racialisation is the natural order. So even in her attempts to change, to change the minds of the speakers in the white conversation, there is an acceptance of group identity that creates a faultline in the project's potential to transcend a 'white' point of view. Krog writes (2009: 132) about her meeting with Mrs Konile:

> There was an uncrossable wall between Mrs Konile and myself. What on earth could I [Antjie] do so that I did not remind her of the white perpetrators as they sat at the Truth Commission hearings with their cruel uncaring and furies? How could I move beyond whiteness towards her... The language sorted out all attempts to hide the differences. Within the language a new hierarchy was established and I was nobody. I came with them. I had no power. I had no control. And to both my delight and anger, neither of my colleagues even once tried to interpret anything to me or include me in the discussion. For them it was unimportant that I should understand what was happening. They didn't even look my way.

In this meeting (which is not really a meeting, as I have already shown), Krog's co-researchers do not interpret or translate; and here is a moment when the conflicting desires of the project come into stark focus. To Mrs Konile, and to Ratele and Mpolweni, it is 'unimportant' that the white woman understands. It is not just that they forget, or that it slips their minds, I want to suggest. What is important here is something crucial to my argument about the labour performed in translation: translation can risk placing the uncomprehending white observer inside a conversation where others might prefer not to look her way.

In her conversation with Nosisi Mpolweni, Mrs Konile says: 'No, I did not have a soft spot for the Boers, even now I do not have a soft spot with the Boers.' The translated words are interesting – a soft spot 'for' and a soft spot 'with' Boers. The text does not comment on this choice of prepositions, which in Xhosa would be rendered differently and would reveal additional meanings that might explain more about how Mrs Konile positions herself with regard to the Boers. Krog does not hear these words (how Mrs Konile is positioned for and with Boers), because she is no longer seated there (she is looking around because no one looks her way), but also because she does not understand Mrs Konile.

> I, [Antjie] was sitting at the table and after the ancestry had been es-
> tablished, I had no idea what they were talking about. The tape was
> running smoothly. Initially I was wondering whether it was possible
> to introduce me in a way that my ancestors could also form an inter-
> connection, but then decided rather to make myself useful by jotting
> down notes about the inside of the room.

In a reflection on the visit, Krog reads the transcript of the conversation
between Mrs Konile, Ratele and Mpolweni. Presumably Mpolweni has
translated it, and it is this English language version that Krog has read – a
version that invites her 'in', but at the same time performs, for her, her
exclusion from the actual conversation. She finds that she is talked about,
not talked to, when she reads what Mrs Konile said about Boers. Mrs
Konile spoke about Boers while Krog was sitting there, not being looked
at. In Krog's response, she decides that Mrs Konile's words about Boers
apply to her, Antjie. Mrs Konile does not name Krog as a Boer. Krog
herself does it in her reading of Mrs Konile's words:

> Every time I [Antjie] read the passages where Mrs Konile rejects the
> Boers, I feel strangely unsettled. She said it during the interview while
> I was sitting with her in her house. Her treatment of me was impec-
> cable: not hostile, not too friendly, as if I was just a person who simply
> did not understand Xhosa... What do I do with my desire that she
> should have another kind of Boer face in her mind's eye? What is
> the difference between forgiveness and saying that you are sorry? A
> neutral academic study does not have the space in which to say that
> you are deeply sorry for what your people and, through them, you
> yourself, did to her, to her life and those of the people she loves. Am I
> out of my mind, I wonder? If I wanted to ask forgiveness it should be
> because I could not speak Xhosa (2009: 197-8).

There are important reasons for someone like Krog (and someone like
me) to learn Xhosa (or any of the other South African languages). But the
learning of Xhosa is not in itself a guarantee that she/we will be looked
at; in fact one can imagine this same conversation, with Krog being able
to follow every word, and still being treated with indifference. In a book
that argues so powerfully for the importance of dialogue not in English,
this may seem a contradictory statement. The point of it is that it is not
only language facility that places Krog (and me, and some readers of this
book) outside the room, or outside Mrs Konile's gaze. What is clear is

Krog's need to be seen and recognised. This recognition she desires is as follows: she wishes to be identified as/with the Boers, and then she wants Mrs Konile to see that she is not like these Boers. In other words, the recognition she wants/needs for the category of white Boer to stay in place, so that she can retain her kinship ties. But she wants Mrs Konile to see her, Krog, as someone who can remain loyal to these kinship ties to her Boer identity and at the same time recognise her as someone who is *not like* the Boers whose faces are in Mrs Konile's mind. In this sense, then, Mrs Konile is the one who is meant to be learning something, learning a lesson.

Kopano Ratele, like Nosisi Mpolweni, reads Krog's 'white conversation' at the inaugural meeting of the project, and agrees to become a member of the team. In what seems like a companion piece, he writes a 'possible black conversation'. At first glance it would seem that there is symmetry: a white author writes a white dialogue, a black author writes a black dialogue. But Ratele's conversation is not that, not the other side. Instead, in it he begins to develop a position which wants to interrogate the very assumptions of the two colour-coded conversations, and also to comment on the ways in which the 'black conversation' is overheard and overlooked by a 'white conversation' which acts like a huge set of quotation marks. In this reading I want to give prominence to the comments on overlooking and overhearing in Ratele's text.

In the chapter which describes 'The Visit', the reader overhears a conversation between the researchers. It is a conversation that is recorded almost by chance, merely to familiarise themselves with the equipment they have borrowed from the university. On the way to meeting Mrs Konile, the researchers try out their recording equipment, and get involved in an argument about the conflict between kinship ties (a topic that is very important during the visit) and apartheid. In this conversation, Krog is concerned with a topic that she returns to over and over in her work – how to be South African and be connected to the unweeping Afrikaner 'men of [her] race' (Krog 1998) at the same time. In his response Ratele says what it means for him to have this version of whiteness quoted, brought up as a topic of conversation.

Before they arrive at Mrs Konile's house, before the meeting in which Krog is not seen and does not take part as listener or speaker, she asks Ratele to explain to her why colour (that is, race) overrides his sense of *ubuntu*. Ratele replies:

> Because white people have hurt black people – so in one sense we are never free of white people. You cannot express your whole self.

Ubuntu bakho. You can't do what is right, because white people simply don't get it, so all the time I have to be myself within a hegemony that is not even aware where I am from ... Let me tell you, whatever you say or do as a black person, you feel it, you feel it here, at the back, just below the shoulder blade, the white voice, always judging. You feel the white eyes on your back wanting you to give an answer that will always either allow them to put their judgement of you on hold, or destroy you in their eyes. Those eyes come from everywhere (2009: 128-9).

This passage develops a way of understanding the relationship between the white gaze and the black gaze (the eyes that do not 'even look my way' in Krog's words). What Ratele describes is the result of the inequalities in society, historical and present, that mean that a black person is always already inserted in a set of white quotation marks. The labour needed to be performed is the erasure, the removal of this imagined (by which I do not mean not-real) eyes and voice. In other words, while Krog wishes Mrs Konile to see her, what Mrs Konile might need is precisely not to have to think about what Krog might need. The labour to be performed is not for Mrs Konile to change, to be translated, so that Krog can feel comfortable. Instead, the critical project is to imagine a context and a discourse where what Krog (and I) feel and desire is not always already the dominant discourse (there are readers to whom this very argument, these very words, will be yet another example of exactly this need to be seen and heard). Then there are the different ways in which the phrase *ubuntu* is used in South African popular discourse. When some people use the phrase, what they mean to invoke is a sense of self-forgiveness and an easy distancing from the past – we are all part of one nation now, we are all entitled to this thing called *ubuntu*. There are other, more historically and linguistically informed responses to *ubuntu*, which want to understand the term not as something to which everyone is entitled. When Ratele uses the phrase '*ubuntu bakho*' (rather than saying 'your *ubuntu*'), he keeps the possessive pronoun untranslated. This linguistic marker shows that *ubuntu* is something not so readily translated and shared, that there are histories and positions that determine which *ubuntu* one is invoking. When Krog calls on Ratele to explain his understanding of *ubuntu*, she is asking him to answer as a black man, to assume the position of the black man. Being invited to explain oneself in this way places Ratele within the quotation marks of a white conversation, or at the very least a racialised conversation, and this is what he wants to resist.

Ratele concludes (2009: 129) his part of the conversation (or the transcript of the conversation, the recording that was meant to try out the equipment) with this statement:

> We never had the space as black people to tell the truth to each other and to reconcile with ourselves, with who we are, also to reconcile with ourselves as our own enemies. Now whiteness literally surrounds us and we never had a chance to say: so here are some white people, how do we interact with them? We have never asked ourselves that question without losing ourselves.

Here is a powerful argument for why Mrs Konile's gaze and hospitality must not be turned in the direction of Krog (or me), because as soon as she does that a set of quotation marks appear that place her in a conversation which has started without her. As soon as she starts to perform the labour of translating herself to me, for me, she risks being contained within the quotation marks of that initial white conversation and within whiteness and its desire to be seen and to be given recognition and forgiveness. It is the primacy given to the white conversation in the text that perhaps irritates Ratele in the final dialogue entry in the text (an irritated exchange to which I return) and which leads him to categorise the white desires and comments as outside the transcript of the joint project.

After the visit to Mrs Konile we read about Ratele's response to it:

> While walking there, Kopano remarked that Mrs Konile on one level reminded him of all the older women he knew who struggled to raise children. 'I can make sense of it because it doesn't make sense, precisely because it doesn't make sense, precisely because there is such a lot of sedimentation in black life in this country. On another level it feels to me that, to use Claude Lanzmann's expression, "the obscenity of understanding", I have to refuse to understand what has happened to her. It is through hanging on to this non-understanding that I will keep being engaged with her and keep believing that what had happened to her is not, and should never ever be, in the realm of human understanding.'

He does this in relation to Mrs Konile's testimony, but also in relation to the text and positions occupied by the Krog signature. The final words of the co-authored text stage for us a disagreement between Ratele and

Krog, in which he insists on being 'angry'. This anger is linked to his insistent non-comprehension. In other words, he wants to insist that sometimes there is no equivalence, and that sometimes it is preferable that not everyone understands. In an earlier section, in the chapter called 'The goat', Ratele asks the reader to imagine explicitly another form of quotation , one that shares many themes with the argument of my book. The reader is presented with the example of the experience of 'most African students, from rural areas or townships, who come into contact with the discipline of psychology at South African universities'. In this example Ratele is possibly telling a story about himself as a student who came to such a university, but also a story about himself as a university teacher who now represents and teaches in a department of Psychology. Students such as those he presents to the reader 'at first appear terribly confused' (2009: 59):

> What confuses them? Well, we teach students to get rid of everything they have been taught about the nature of social relations, about themselves, and about other people. If the students do not quickly shed their notions about what a person is and how people relate to each other, they are bound to struggle and, in fact, drop out ... What students from rural areas or townships have to learn in the very first week of their studies in order to stand a chance of mastering their new world is that they cannot regard their teachers as their 'fathers' or 'mothers', 'ooms' and 'tannies'. In other words, they have to un-learn one of the central lessons they have been taught from their earli-est moments in most of their families: that any older person is their *mme* or *nkgono* (mother or grandmother), *ntate* or *ntatemoholo* (fa-ther or grandfather), or *abuti* or *ausi* (brother or sister). They have to turn away from the lesson they received at home that any person of a similar age was their sibling (*ngwaneso* or *kgaeitsedi*). This has far-reaching implications for how someone learns, and in turn, for whether they pass or fail.

What Ratele describes is a student who is expected to refashion herself by entering the university (the place of the conversations that will lead to this book *There was this Goat*). He wants the reader of the book to remember the expectations of the place where the book comes from; and he wants this place to remember where students come from. He wants, in the terminology of my own project, for the accent of the student to remain audible, and to be part of the university's response to her.

Here the images of learning and teaching take on their most literal meanings, when one thinks about this context, the university. In Ratele's sections in the book, there is an insistence on difference, differences of opinion, differences of position and experience; and on anger and resistance. When agreement is reached, he cautions that agreement might well lead to the silencing or muting of one of the points of the disagreement or difference. The TRC has often been understood in this way, as a muting of difference and grievance; but Ratele does not make this connection explicitly.

Conversations can be understood as forms of 'transcript' in which the hearer/translator/transcriber is either more or less attuned to the speaker's words and actions. It is easy to see why conversations that assume insurmountable difference cannot lead to a meaningful transcript; but Ratele's sections are also interested in the transcript that wants to mute difference and neutralise accents. Ratele wants to insist on his own inability to understand Mrs Konile, and this non-understanding from him is significantly different from the non-understanding in the white conversation. For the white conversation, Mrs Konile is 'white noise' (and reading in a South African accent these metaphorical uses of white and black always bring with them particular histories, always yield more meaning than they may have intended); for Ratele to say he understands her is to assume that all black conversations are the same. Ratele wants to insist on the differences *within* the black conversation, but he also wants to empty out the sameness that Krog – at times – wants to insert into the white conversation. This is the premise of their disagreement at the end of the text (the final transcript of the co-research). Of course the three authors must have agreed on the final text, but in the Krog section there is a staged dialogue that, for Ratele, is not part of the transcript of the project, it is a transcript of the Antjie that is interested in and invested in whiteness. In response to this dialogue, he suggests Krog is collapsing into whiteness and thereby (as she provides evidence of the existence of the one 'good', transformed, white person) divesting him of his right to be angry, an anger that can be read as a performance of non-understanding.

The Krog texts develop a theory of witnessing and translation that is explored in greater detail in Krog's other works (and in particular in *Begging to Be Black*): translation as a way of becoming someone other, of imagining the position of the other. The Ratele sections develop a position that is not wholly unfamiliar to debates about translation either; he wants to insist on the untranslatability of some discourses, and the need to retain difference. The text stages a number of arguments between these two positions and persons, what is the 'value' of translation: for whose benefit it is done, who does the work, what is gained and what is lost.

The final transcript is that of a conversation between the three researchers, and the topic is once again *ubuntu* and how to understand the self. The research project (the official transcript and its various retranslations and reinterpretations, as well as what has been learnt) is summarised in this conversation. Ratele says:

> To ask how the self is formed, to ask about borders, are the wrong questions. You should ask, what is the self in the family? Within the networks, the map of networks, where is the dot that is you? There is no dot without a connecting line. The self is a combination of things that are connecting. When the lines are removed there is no self. That is the troubling thing. It is as if I want to pull back, I don't want these lines connecting me. Part of me cannot run away from them, they are the me (2009: 204).

This very last transcribed conversation concerns the status of the research, what it was/is, and whether (and when) it became 'something else'. This can be understood in a number of ways – in particular since the stated aim of the project has been change and transformation. What this transformation is to be, to whose benefit and with which audience in mind, is what the authors ultimately want to clarify for themselves and one another. And it is in the discussion of whether the project, the book itself, did change into something else that the final disagreement is staged and transcribed:

> ANTJIE: I feel bereft of an opportunity to be a person to her, to pre-sent to her some other kind of whiteness.
> KOPANO: Now, that is not a person who is part of this team talking. That is the Antjie in you that speaks. Or let me re-phrase: it is the white Antjie in you that speaks.
> ANTJIE: What's your problem? Didn't you say in your 'First Black' and 'Second Black' conversation that you would like whites to ask for forgiveness?
> KOPANO: The problem is this. I am angry at white people. Very angry. Because they refuse to acknowledge how much they have benefited from their whiteness. But we have interacted with you as an individual, a person, and on that basis we have negotiated and

become simply human beings with one another. But the moment you decide you want to become the collective white and want to act on behalf of the whites, you blunt my anger.

ANTJIE: But isn't that exactly what I should be doing?

KOPANO: No, because my anger should not be blunted until white people in general have changed, and not because one white person has become a person for me.

ANTJIE: I don't understand. Black people are proud of their interconnectedness, their collectiveness, and yet you don't think it is precisely my Africanness that makes me feel collective with Afrikaners.

These words, to Ratele, place Krog outside the team, outside the Krog ~ Mpolweni ~ Ratele kinship. It is a disagreement that can be understood as a key moment in the text; and I want to suggest that this disagreement, and the transcript of the disagreement, is an excellent example of accented thinking. It provides a version of teaching and learning, of reading and writing, that resists understanding. In other words, it provides us with a version of the ways in which, in a university setting, non-understanding can be theorised and not papered over. The fact that the text is co-authored makes it, even as visual artefact, a transcript of a 'conversation', an explicit example of not-sameness. In addition, the disagreements between the authors rehearse the process of transcription and how transcription (what survives, what is lost) is theorised throughout the text.

The co-authored text ends with a disagreement, and it is a disagreement in which the authors are in conflict over the meaning of their work. It is a disagreement about what one might call, in other contexts, 'agreement'. Ratele is commenting on the fact that Krog is collapsing into a position from where she assumes herself to be a representative of whites, an interlocutor in a white conversation. The white conversation and the black conversation, despite the parallel in their names, are lacking in symmetry. The black conversation thematises the fact that it risks being absorbed into, distorted by, overheard by, has historically been circumscribed by, the white conversation. And hence the black conversation includes in it an awareness of questions of audience and location that is perhaps exactly what the 'white conversation' lacks. Krog wants to renounce her whiteness (or at least a particular kind of whiteness), but precisely in order to recover another understanding of whiteness. She is begging to be black, but she wants to be and remain an Afrikaner woman who begs to be (seen as, invited in as) black. Ratele wants not to have to imagine this other, wants to get to a position where the spectre of the encapsulating white gaze does not determine what things can mean. And he wants not to have to 'see' her desire to be seen.

In the possible black conversation (2009: 32), Second Black says:

> To truly hear Mrs K's truth, and the truth of the black people who testified at the Truth Commission hearings, you have to work hard to understand it, you have to gain our trust. It's not going to be given to you just like that, because you may turn and use it against us, as happened many, many times under apartheid. Don't you know that? I think most of us know it. And most of those who went to the Truth Commission knew that before they arrived, or soon realised that the truth and reconciliation in the Commission were sham performances.

While Second Black's words cannot be conflated with Ratele's (as First White and Second White similarly ought not in a simple way to be confused with Krog), the comments here about a 'you' turning against 'us' are significant. At issue here are forms of communication where someone ('you') has been let in, and has been extended a hand of welcome and trust. The suspicion is that 'you' will turn and use this 'against us'. This is a strand in some arguments against translation, and the need to keep communication within the group and not accessible to outsiders, (especially outsiders who may be hostile to its contents). Developing these insights brings one to the central issue of the nature of the different forms of not-understanding in the book. Not being understood, not wanting to be understood, can be a choice made in order to keep some things hidden or untranslated. In the conclusion I return to these questions of understanding and not-understanding through a reading of the final chapter of James C Scott's work on hidden transcripts, *Domination and the Arts of Resistance*, in which he writes of the rupturing event when the hidden transcript is spoken.

Being understood, one sees, is to run the risk of being transcribed, and in particular transcribed inaccurately; it is to run the risk of having someone else's desires become the quotation marks around your words. In Krog's texts there often appear white characters who speak African languages, a policeman or farmer who 'speaks Xhosa like a Xhosa'. Yet linguistic proficiency does not prove affiliation. They may be instances of speech that are part of a white conversation. In other words, it is even possible for a white person to speak Xhosa like a Xhosa as part of a white conversation.

So when Krog writes that she was meant to ask forgiveness for not speaking Xhosa, it is worth remembering that it is possible to learn a language without that necessarily shifting the 'conversation'. Similarly, Krog's title *Begging to be Black* wants to hold on to 'blackness' as not different from itself. The risks of essentialism, of nativism, are inherent in this position. For Krog wants to retain her Afrikaans-speaking, Boer (more specific than white) identification, but through begging to be black and asking forgiveness for not speaking Xhosa (*A Change of Tongue* as another of her titles has it), to transform this category of origin.

The text shows an engagement with misunderstood and mistranscribed testimony, and I have argued that this co-authored text is itself an example of this. In this multivoiced text there is a return to a position of and insistence on non-understanding (in the sense of finding exact equivalence). It is illuminating to think of this together with another strand in the text, the strand that relates to questions of pedagogy. The location of the dialogue, and the location of the attempted re-transcription, is the university. But the text also invites an engagement with the role of learning and teaching, and the benefit and gain to be derived to those involved in the activities. When Krog says: 'I want white people to learn', Ratele might answer: now that very desire is an interference, that wish places the white desire in the room again. Krog needs Mrs Konile to address her, to hear her – to bridge the gap. Instead Ratele wants to emphasise the gap, and to keep it there – to retain the accentedness of his understanding of *ubuntu bakho*.

Chapter 3

NJABULO NDEBELE'S
ORDINARY ADDRESS

IN this chapter, accent is understood in the most literal way, as it refers to the varieties of English spoken by South Africans. Accentedness and lack of accentedness are themes running through the work of Njabulo Ndebele, considered by many to be the leading intellectual in South Africa today. He has published some highly acclaimed fiction (in particular *Fools* and *The Cry of Winnie Mandela*), but it is his cultural and literary essay collections, *Rediscovery of the Ordinary* (1991, 1994 and 2006) and *Fine Lines from the Box* (2007) that have come to have the greatest influence. Many of the pieces collected in *Rediscovery of the Ordinary* and in *Fine Lines from the Box* were delivered as addresses and lectures, and contain traces of and references to the particular contexts for which they were written and where they were delivered. Repeatedly, one sees Ndebele drawing attention to the fact that every speech utterance is the activation of intertextual fields. The second volume of essays contains a rather shocking postscript by a South African academic, Tlhalo Raditlhalo. Raditlhalo has written elsewhere on the effects of exile on South Africa's literary traditions, and his approach to literary history is a good example of the accented scholarship about which this book theorises. Being invited to contribute a piece on Njabulo Ndebele's work, writes Raditlhalo, was 'the culmination of a dream long harboured' (2007: 257). Yet, contrasted with this statement of a dream long dreamt and now about to come true, is another anecdote which at first reading seems perplexing. It is a story of silence and misperception, of lack of trust in his audience. Raditlhalo (2007: 257) begins:

> Sometime in the 2004 academic year I presented a seminar reading in the Department of English Language and Literature at the University of Cape Town where I teach ... During question time, a colleague of mine, having noted the respect I conferred in my talk on Ntate Mphahlele, asked me who I thought had inherited his mettle as humanist public intellectual. I unhesitatingly responded that Professor Njabulo S Ndebele was the godson and that no one approximated Mphahlele's incisive intellectual engagement with the same degree of reflexivity as Ndebele.
>
> My response was followed by an awkward silence during which the questioner smiled (I honestly cannot decide whether this was sympathetic or condescending) and, since there was no follow-up question, I did not elaborate. I am reminded of this occasion, however, and am very glad of the opportunity to follow up my answer here, having been asked to write an appreciation of this collection of Ndebele's essays.

I want to underline two themes in this unusual introduction to his Afterword, which is, after all, meant to be a celebration. The first of these is affiliation, the second mistrust. In the reading I want to give of Njabulo Ndebele's work, my argument is informed by Raditlhalo's insights and the tradition in which he places and reads Ndebele, and in my argument intertextuality is seen as a version of accentedness; in making decisions about which intertextual links one invokes in reading a text, one is making decisions about the 'accent' of the work. How intertextuality functions in ways that resemble kinship and affiliation is clear; a text has meaning and resonance through how it is read with, and alongside, other texts. More surprising is the way in which mistrust and suspicion can be related to intertextuality, as I show in the discussion of Raditlhalo's piece.

Raditlhalo sets the scene in a university seminar – as it happens, the university where Njabulo Ndebele is at that time the vice-chancellor. Yet this seminar is shown to be home, and also not home, to his argument. The seminar, on the 'intricacies and frustrations [he] encountered while editing a *festschrift* devoted to the South African intellectual elder Professor Es'kia Mphahlele' (2007: 257), is a reflection on the work he has done, the challenges he has faced when celebrating and evaluating the work of another intellectual elder. One would imagine that this occasion (a recently arrived academic giving a seminar on an important project) could be one full of pride and a sense of achievement. But this is not the way Raditlhalo recounts it.

His affiliation in the seminar is not with his colleagues (a seminar as a way for a department to build cohesion, to knit together research and personal interests). He demonstrates instead a connection with his subject in opposition to one with his colleagues. He refers to Mpahlele as *ntate*, literally 'father', but *ntate* is a term that carries here more than the connotation of an older person worthy of respect. In this context, Raditlhalo is also stressing his untranslated relationship to Mphahlele ('*ntate*' not 'father' or the previously used 'professor'), a gesture towards a certain kind of human intertextual placement. The choice of term of respect places Mphahlele's worth outside English, and beyond the reaches of the room – a seminar room in the English Department of an English language university. Raditlhalo's choice of this term of respect is meant to evoke for a listener a context other than this seminar room; but it also betrays a suspicion that he will not be heard in the way he wants to be – or at least he wants to foreground this possibility.

When Raditlhalo finishes his talk, we read, there follows the customary question time. Raditlhalo is asked the question about inheritance, about affiliation and influence. And he writes that his response to the question is unhesitating. This account of the decisive, unhesitating response is followed – we read in Raditlhalo's version – by 'an awkward silence' on the part of his listeners. Whether others in the room would describe the silence as 'awkward' or not awkward (or even remember it as a silence at all) is not the point; the point is that Raditlhalo has made a certain kind of argument (about affiliation, about context, about the challenges of reading in a certain way, about the inheritance of intellectual traditions), and to him 'awkward silence' would in fact be the *appropriate* and even the desired response from this particular room. It would be appropriate because it would be an acknowledgement of the ways in which the room (and these seminars are normally held in what is called the 'tea-room', a room that displays and performs particular histories of social interaction, the format of this seminar, the institutional setting and its implicit and explicit exclusions) cannot contain what he has had to say; and perhaps also that the tradition he has imagined is one that has not been spoken about in this room in the way he has done. When the questioner smiles at his response, we have only Raditlhalo's interpretation of the encounter – and even *he* writes that he 'honestly cannot decide whether this was sympathetic or condescending'. What is it that makes this smile so unreadable to him, what makes him unable 'honestly' to accept a colleague's smile as one of agreement and admiration, as acknowledgment of the worth of a valued colleague?

The interpretation (that is, the interpretation of the inability to interpret) I want to try out is that this account of Raditlhalo's 'honest' incomprehension is not merely his anecdotal way of introducing his essay and defending his project. I want to suggest that the incomprehension (and the account of the incomprehension, the insistence on it) is a central part of Raditlhalo's project, and is also a suggestive way of approaching the project of Njabulo Ndebele. My argument is that this mistrust of a smile (and also to have one's smile so distrusted, and to think through what this means) is a version of the activist work of accented thinking.

Raditlhalo suspects that the intertextual field, the tradition he has outlined in his seminar on Mphahlele, is one to which he feels more affiliated than do others in the room. He also intends to show that he feels more affiliation with the subject of his seminar than he does with his colleagues. He asserts that the reading he has done, as well as the writing, shapes and is part of a tradition unlike those traditions already demonstrated and respected in the room. By insisting on the unreadability of the smile (and the questioner's intent), Raditlhalo means to underline the ways in which what he has to say is not historically 'at home' in the seminar room, or the university. (It is worth adding here that, for the argument I make, it is not relevant whether this mistrust is well-founded. It is easy to slip into a position where one starts to defend the department, or the seminar series, or feels tempted to bring out old course descriptions to prove that his mistrust is unfounded and that this department has all along been 'home' to ideas such as this.) My way of reading this anecdote about mistrust is instead to take it as a model for how to read Ndebele: with an eye open for scenes of mistrust and suspicion, and how mistrust and the performance of mistrust can function as a way towards the accented reading and writing practices my book seeks to develop.

In the discussion of Njabulo Ndebele's critical work, I trace some of the implications of how his work has been read, contextually and intertextually; in other words, the level of accentedness one can find in the readings. Ndebele's essays have been collected in two volumes, so in the first place the coherence of a single-author volume brings certain themes to the fore. In this reading, one is automatically on the lookout for intertextuality *within* his work, and the reader seeks out clusters of ideas around the context of utterances. Many of the articles are written versions of lectures and speeches, providing a way of thinking about context and audience. In the reception of the work (the way it has been read, and the texts against and alongside which it has been read), there is another way of demonstrating the way contextualisation affects the work of a text. Instead of seeing intertextuality as a form of affiliation and affinity, what I show here is that explicit references to intertextuality can be used to demonstrate *lack* of affinity. Intertextuality in the work of Ndebele is often asserted or denied in contexts of mistrust and suspicion, and typically functions as a way of resisting containment. In other words, Ndebele's writings and lectures provide us with examples of utterances that work towards asserting and maintaining a certain set of intertexts and contexts, and *not* being absorbed by another set.

One way of approaching this aspect of his work might be to refer to orality and its insistence on context, something which is of course rendered differently when a text circulates in written form. We are reading a written version, and the written text's intertextual field is potentially very different from that of the oral version, the speech, as new intertextual fields are activated by the context of publication, and then by where and how readers read the text. In Ndebele's lectures and speeches we find frequent reference to the fact that he is addressing divided audiences – audiences with differing assumptions and values. He makes explicit what this book wants to seek out and to develop: an awareness of the different contexts within and to which we speak. One way in which this is developed is through his comments on 'English'. In no speech is this more evident than in 'The English language and social change in South Africa', a text that can still shock in its incisive exposition of the suspicions it harbours about the intentions of its host, the English Academy of South Africa, and its audience. This speech was delivered as 'the keynote address ... at the Jubilee Conference of the English Academy of South Africa; Johannesburg, September, 1986, many years before the first democratic elections (*English Academy Review* 1987). The tone is one of suspicion and mistrust, and its theme can be read as that of refusing a particular context and set of intertextual assumptions, and resisting the kind of absorption that neutralises the meanings of one's words.

Before discussing Ndebele's response to the invitation to give this significant speech, it is worth examining the history of the host, and context for first publication of this speech, The English Academy of

South Africa. The Academy was founded in 1961, and is still the only academy in the world for the English language. To anyone familiar with South Africa's history, 1961 will resonate as a year in which English was being endangered by Afrikaans, the National Party's official language, after the country became a republic. It is also one year after the Sharpeville massacre, and the year that all black political organisations in South Africa were outlawed. The English Academy of South Africa was thus founded at a moment when English seemed under threat from the new hegemony of the National Party and Afrikaans. There is another context, and that is the assertion of a link with England, an attempt at maintaining a connection in the face of political developments in South Africa. Significant here, though, is the lack of an awareness of the already lively debates about English in Africa, or a context that places South African English alongside other South African languages.

In 1983, the Academy (still using the Tudor Rose as its emblem) started to publish a journal, the *English Academy Review*. A review is, of course, a name for a certain kind of academic journal; but it is clear from the first few volumes of the publication that the editors also intended it to act as a 'review' of the role and ideals of the English Academy, with which they seemed to be at odds. The review included a range of papers that place English in South Africa in the context of African languages debates; two major papers by Es'kia Mphahlele were included, for example, both discussing the ownership and political uses of English within its African contexts (see Mphahlele 1984 and 1985). Yet printed at the back of each review were included the minutes and annual reports of the Academy, written as if the speakers had not read the rest of the volume, nor taken note of its content.

One unintentionally ludicrous item from the annual report of 1983 (the first year of the review's publication) serves to illustrate this point:

> To complete the picture as far as our specifically language-related activities are concerned: we were represented at a 'Military Language Congress' organised by the SA Defence Force at Voortrekkerhoogte, in May this year; we have finally won our battle to have the 'equals' sign banished when a word is broken at the end of a line – the hyphen is back, in both English and Afrikaans (*English Academy Review* 1983: 125).

This victory shows no awareness that the South African Defence Force was considered by many South Africans at the time as an agent of civil war. This small paragraph reveals a great deal about the agenda set by the Academy, and the contexts in which it saw itself.

Ndebele was invited by this body to give its jubilee lecture, and took as one of the structuring themes a close reading of the English Academy of South Africa's mission statement. He read the invitation intertextually with what he had already read coming from the Academy, and in his speech laid out the reasons for his mistrust of the very invitation to him to speak. If the invitation were written in the same 'language' as the rest of the Academy's documents, then he needed to interpret it with caution and mistrust, for the invitation from this intertextual field could not possibly be welcoming of what he had to say. His position on English could not be brought in relation to the ways in which the South African Defence Force used the hyphen in their written documents; there is no intertextual work that can assert affiliation. And so Ndebele's speech can be read as an exploration of intertextuality and its political weight; and at the same time as an assertion of the intertextual field he wants to maintain by holding on to a position of mistrust and suspicion.

The English Academy of South Africa, we read with Ndebele, is an association dedicated to 'promoting the effective use of English as a dynamic language in Southern Africa. Membership is open to all persons and organisations identifying with the Academy's mission and sharing its vision.' Thus the organisation stresses 'openness', but it is an openness that comes with a border guard: the need to identify with and share the vision. The mission statement does not say that one has to be a mother tongue speaker, but it does say that one has to speak 'effective' English. The test for this is unclear; what Ndebele suspects, however, is that he is not being invited to address this body because it intends to broaden its definition of effectiveness, dynamism or vision; he suspects he is being invited in order to make *him* conform, to contain his difference and neutralise his accentedness.

Perhaps the key statement in this address is a direct commentary on the Academy's intentions in inviting him to be their 'keynote' speaker:

> Practically, this need to maintain control over English by its native speakers has given birth to a policy of manipulative open-mindedness in which it is held that English belongs to all who use it provided that it is used correctly. It is assumed, of course, that it is the native speakers who will determine the standards of correctness (1991: 101).

At issue here is what recurs in almost every one of the essays in the collection *Rediscovery of the Ordinary*, a reflection on the language of the encounter, and the negotiations around which language is being used to interpret the encounter. In this lecture, Ndebele addresses explicitly the guardians of the English language in South Africa, in a highly political move which critiques its very invitation to him to speak. He accepts the invitation and prepares a speech to give at the meeting, but then uses his speech to insist on deciding the terms of his presence there himself, and of giving voice to his mistrust of their ostensibly good intentions.

Ndebele says:

> [I]t should be clear that much of the talk about reform and change, from the point of view of white South Africa in general, is premised not on what the whites of South Africa may have to unlearn, but on what black people, those 'prospective citizens of the Republic', need to be speedily introduced to so that they can become 'responsible' citizens of the future; so that they can become westerners in black skins (1991: 108).

At issue here is the English language and its uses, but it is also an argument about the way values and standards are determined. In the mission statement of the Academy, Ndebele finds evidence that all 'change' is to happen at the address of black South Africans, to become more worthy of being speakers of English. About white South Africans he says that '[u]nfortunately, whites are not present while these significant changes [to black South Africans' sense of themselves] are taking place' (1991: 110), and later, 'it cannot be taken for granted that whatever white South Africans have to offer is inherently valuable' (1991: 111). These comments are made on the level of language (ownership of English, the changes in the nature and role of South African English). But it also refers to the nature of conversation, and who gets to determine the terms of communication. The paper ends with the revealing phrase: 'The aim of this paper was to seize the opportunity to present and formulate the problems from the perspective that I have adopted' (1991: 117). It is this 'perspective' that I want to emphasise, and that is central to Ndebele's cultural programme. It is a 'perspective' that insists on voicing its mistrust, and on deciding the terms of its own presence. Ndebele's perspective is an example of what I have called accented thinking, a way of approaching encounters like this with suspicion and resistance.

The lecture is first published in the *English Academy Review*, and then, some years later, republished in Ndebele's *Rediscovery of the Ordinary: Essays on South African Literature and Culture*. In the Preface to the collection, Ndebele sets out his project, which is to answer a question: '[W]ith the demise of grand apartheid now [in 1991, after the release of Nelson Mandela and the unbanning of the ANC, and after the addresses and papers in the collection were written] certain, what are South African writers now going to write about?' (1991: 7). He points to the contradictions and difficulties of interpreting the actions of the National Party, an 'undesirable government being seen to be performing some desired functions'. Ndebele is here talking about the disjunction between the origin, the address, the *signature* of the action (the National Party, custodians and defenders of grand apartheid), and the action itself – the unbanning of the ANC and the seeming willingness to enter into dialogue. His point is that utterances made by the National Party need to be responded to with mistrust and suspicion; one has to listen to and to read these statements intertextually, insisting on the history and traditions that inform them. The National Party government has positioned itself 'somewhere within the ethical domain of the liberation movement, with rather confusing results', and so, he writes, 'what are we to make of them'? (1991: 8).

The point Ndebele is making is that the utterance and the signature appended to it do not rhyme, and that for him, the one to whom the utterance is addressed, there is an incomprehensibility at the heart of the communication. Something is being said, but the address seems to be performing an action other than that which is explicitly stated. He continues, developing this strand of thinking: 'The fact of the matter is that the liberation movement has been denied the ultimate experience: to witness the resounding defeat of an enemy. The Bastille has not been stormed. There have been no enemy soldiers withdrawing in disarray. Such a situation could possibly have made more easily visible the need for fresh beginnings without the confusing cobwebs of the past interfering. It would seem, therefore, that the terrible spectacle of apartheid oppression seems destined to end in a comparatively non-spectacular, yet essential process of negotiation. This situation will be extremely demanding on our capacity to know and understand what is going on' (1991: 9). This is the project Ndebele sets himself, to develop an approach that can decode the 'illusion' of communication. Elsewhere, he writes about FW de Klerk as 'masked' (2009: 64), and of celebratory fireworks displays as a way of obscuring communication (2007: 23). By collecting together these scattered references one can build up an argument around communication that misfires, and a conversational contract in which there has been a breach by one of the parties – and for Ndebele this breach is the fact that one party to the conversation attempts to control the terms of the encounter. What he wishes to do is to draw attention to the breach, and to insist on the worth of being a suspicious reader, alert to which intertexts are activated and which silenced.

Apart from Ndebele's speech on the English language, his most influential paper is the title essay of the collection: 'The rediscovery of the ordinary: Some new writings in South Africa'. This piece had been delivered as a lecture, the keynote address to the conference 'New Writing in Africa: Continuity and Change' in London in 1984. I want to show how Ndebele's understanding of 'ordinary' can be read within the context of his own body of work and the tradition I am charting for it; and, in contrast, how it has been read in ways that provide other (often neutralising, de-accenting) contexts.

Ndebele's project in this essay is often invoked alongside Albie Sachs's widely circulated and even more widely discussed cultural paper 'Preparing ourselves for freedom', and the two read together as an insistence that art should turn away from the struggle towards themes like love and the everyday. Placing Ndebele in this context, the 'ordinariness' his title refers to is read as a shunning of politics, and many have read Ndebele in this way – either celebrating it or criticising him for betraying another set of ideals. Interestingly, the recuperative, neutralising reading of Ndebele is a very good example of just what he describes in his work. Tlhalo Raditlhalo writes disparagingly of the Sachs paper as a 'now largely irrelevant ANC in-house seminar paper' (2007: 258), and that Ndebele's paper was 'used as cannon fodder in a battle not of his choosing', that he was 'reluctantly yoked to the Sachs position as the debate regarding cultural production in the New South Africa raged' (2007: 258). Ndebele's paper came to be read as a defence of the end to the 'liberation aesthetic' (2007: 258) and even as an end to any political talk. But the context in which Raditlhalo's and my own arguments read Ndebele is one where his 'ordinariness' is defined as a call to a certain kind of activism – a deeply political ordinariness.

Ndebele himself has commented drily on this twinning with Sachs: 'The major controversy around Sachs's paper has tended to focus on why his statement has attracted so much attention, and why other people's similar statements have not. It's not a very important question in my view.

The reception of Albie Sachs's paper indicates that it's important *where* you say something' (Brown and Van Dyk 1991: 49). Ndebele means here that Sachs's statement was made from within the ANC, and addressed to the ANC seminar, while his own has circulated among academics. In the 'Broken gourds' piece, Raditlhalo would want to repeat this gesture, to insist on the difference context makes to one's reading. If read in a certain way, Ndebele's call to ordinariness means that we need to write about love and private life; read within another tradition, and more angrily and more suspiciously *against* other traditions, it becomes instead an insistence on the work that is needed to rediscover traditions that are there but have not been articulated.

In *Fine Lines from the Box* Ndebele develops a set of terms and strategies that have as their themes interdependency and what he calls 'abandoning certitude'. One way of interpreting this abandonment of certitude could be to relate it to the theme of suspicion. Abandoning certitude would then be a form of reading that insists on examining the unspoken assumptions of a text and its contexts. Interdependency has a clear social meaning, but it is also possible to use the word as a way of describing the kind of intertextual work that accented thinking represents.

Whereas *Rediscovery of the Ordinary* was concerned with the risks of recuperation and containment, *Fine Lines from the Box* develops the themes of seeing the communicative act in terms of mutuality (which must not be confused with reconciliation – this mutuality often involves conflict). Ndebele writes here of accepting difference of opinion or perspective, of 'living with disagreement' (2007: 30). His language includes numerous references to attempts at successful, positive, acts of communication: 'interacting identities' (2007: 109), 'common responsibility' (2007: 111), 'locating ourselves within questions posed by others' (2007: 112), 'mutual discovery' (2007: 140), 'mutual vulnerability' (2007: 221), 'abandoning certitude' (2007: 221). This version of communication is not one that tries to prescribe a mode of communication that leaves no ambiguity or misunderstanding (it is assumed that these are built into communication), but what Ndebele's version does insist on is mutuality and interaction. Ndebele is still addressing those who were (perhaps reluctantly, perhaps ignorantly) the 'human point of reference' (2007: 15) in South Africa, but this address is explicitly overwritten with another address, a new 'point of reference'. And, in addition, the address requires of the addressee to perform the work of 'activist understanding' (2007: 11), to do the work that will make it possible to place the utterance within other contexts. This is the interpretation of 'abandoning certitude' that, in Ndebele's argument, can lead to new forms of subjectivity, and new forms of interaction. When he talks of vulnerability as a condition for transformation, it becomes clear that this is a path to what my own book calls 'accenting' our interactions – in the classroom as well as outside it.

When Ndebele writes of 'interacting identities' (2007: 109) he is insisting on the recognition of a lack of separateness, historical and present – a concept also developed by Sarah Nuttall in *Entanglement*. But the word 'interacting' here is not only an adjective describing the kind of identities, it can also be doing the work, be a form of the verb 'interact', here used to show that identity is not something static or complete. In this way, Ndebele aims not only at (re)discovering intellectual traditions, but also explicitly points to the work that needs to be done to make and find intertextual links in communication. In 'Learning to give up certitudes' (a lecture delivered in the USA in 2004), Ndebele (2007: 221) said:

> [A]t the point at which you recognise mutual vulnerability between yourself and an adversary that will not go away, you signal a preparedness to recognise that there might be new grounds for a common humanity, whose promise lies in the real possibility that you may have to give up something of what has defined your reality, handed down from a past that cannot entirely meet your best interests now and in the future. It is the humility that arises when you give up certitudes around what was previously the uncontested terrain of your value system and unsustainable positions derived from it. It is the willingness to embrace vulnerability of the kind that faces you when you learn to unlearn because there is so much more that is new to learn. Your new sense of comfort comes from the confidence that others, who are on the opposite side, are doing so too, and are also experiencing vulnerability.

In this address (a commencement address at Wesleyan University in Middletown, Connecticut on 23 May 2004), Ndebele is speaking as 'a South African who is black, a man, a husband and father, a teacher who has interacted with many students, teachers and researchers over the years' (2007: 218). He reflects on his age compared to that of his listeners' (who are commencing their academic lives), and on the age of democracy in South Africa compared to that in the United States. Being old, he says, is far from the thoughts of young people beginning their adult lives. Yet he asks them to make an imaginative leap, trying to be 'old': 'I would like to invite you to try to be old, not in age, but in the ability to stretch the imagination back into history because I am fascinated by what ten years of one country and more than two hundred years of another means about what could possibly connect them' (2007: 218). And so Ndebele translates into this context his thoughts about interconnectedness and obligation, about imagining the assumptions of one's interlocutor. He asks young students in the United States to imagine themselves old, to imagine a link between their democracy and South Africa's democracy; it is an address that makes much of the differences between the speaker and the addressee, but also asks them to perform a process of translation that brings agreement and an imaginative affiliation. It is precisely through the acknowledgement of the difference between speaker and audience that he makes his point about similarity – or the imaginative work needed to be done in order to find this affiliation.

Vulnerability and unlearning, as examples of 'continuous critical engagement' (2007: 62) are elements in the activism Ndebele wants to develop in readers of his work and listeners to his addresses. In a number of essays and addresses language recurs as an important theme, developing ideas from 'The English language and social change' and his interest in the role and status of African languages. In *Fine Lines from the Box,* in line with Ndebele's strand of mutuality and (un)learning, is an interesting set of references to translation and multilingualism. The clearest example is to be found in 'An encounter with my roots', where Ndebele writes autobiographically about language migration, and the intimate connections between languages and identities. In this essay, he traces his changing relationship to the languages he speaks (Zulu, Sotho, English), and the possibility of writing multilingual works of fiction. 'There are aspects of my experience that I cannot imagine in English,' writes Ndebele. 'This leads me to the conclusion that if my linguistic experience as a South African has grown in, and been influenced by, the intersection of three communities whose respective languages I speak, read, and write (with different levels of capability), I am forced to confront the task of exploring artistic possibilities resident in that intersection' (2007: 151).

In this version of multilingualism, the *intersection* of languages is described as a kind of home, a place where an imagination can be 'resident'. The logic of this insight, that it is possible to live at the inter-section of languages, provides another way of thinking about accented teaching. It is possible to see multilingualism (the ability to read and to live at the intersection between South African languages) as a form of the activist work that my book seeks to describe and theorise. The intersection of contexts and knowledges is also a useful way of approaching classroom encounters. In the accented classroom, the assumptions underlying knowledge are questioned, and the teacher is open to the possibilities of the knowledge and references that the students bring to the material. The teacher's vulnerability is then of a kind that allows her to learn while she teaches and to make the knowledge in the classroom accented in the ways the students need.

It is in 'Iph'indlela: finding a way through confusion', a transcript of the Steve Biko Memorial Lecture given on 12 September 2000, that this theme of living at an intersection is developed more completely. Ndebele (2007: 127) starts, not by explaining (by translating into English) his title, but by describing instead its 'origins':

> There is a small story to the origins of my title. A formidable frustration for most writers is what to do with a blank page. It stares at you with silent, intimidating power. To deal with this situation, I decided to put down words at random ... I leaned back to see if I could spot any emergent trends that would suggest a possible title. I stared at the words and found no sustainable connections to hook onto immediately. But, just as I was about to decide that my random collection of words had not helped, I sat forward as a question formed itself without any effort on my part. I wrote '*Iph'indlela?*' I did, indeed, feel lost. I could find no immediate path through the forest of words.

When the 'silent' page speaks, it speaks of the lack of a road, the uncertainty of a path. But the utterance itself is a form of path, and the language in which the page breaks its silence shows the way by not speaking in English. The last section of the address, to do with finding a way that is not the way of monolingual English, deals with what Ndebele calls a 'critique of whiteness', and the relationship of this whiteness to 'the project of development' (2007: 136). Development is a term with a lively history, particularly where Africa is concerned. But here Ndebele uses the words in an inflected way: to bring it in relation to 'whiteness', and the need for development in this area. Writing of the process of change, or 'development', he writes of the need for mutual, general development:

> On the whole, though, white South Africans will be called upon to make greater adjustments to black needs than the other way around. This is an essential shift in white identity in which 'whiteness' can undergo an experiential transformation by absorbing new cultural experience as an essential condition for achieving a new sense of

cultural rootedness. That is why every white South African should be proud to speak, read, and write at least one African language, and be ashamed if they are not able to (2007: 136).

The road he describes here is the road that will lead to the intersection, to the position from where one can read and hear more than the monolingual voice. It is the road that leads to accented ways of living and teaching – and, perhaps, living at the intersection.

South African whiteness, he continues, needs to 'come out from under the umbrella' of 'international whiteness'. Read against the background of Ndebele's other work, South African whiteness, one could say, needs to 'rediscover' alternative histories and traditions, needs to uncover the connections and intertexts ready to be activated by a particular viewpoint: 'Putting itself at risk, it will have to declare that it is home now, sharing in the vulnerability of other compatriot bodies. South African whiteness will declare that its dignity is inseparable from the dignity of black bodies' (2007: 137). By using a set of rhetorical devices linked to language and multilingualism, Ndebele's thought opens up a rich set of interpretive possibilities. It allows a way of 'seeing' the intertexts of South Africa's racial history, but it also allows a way forward and out of whiteness (and blackness, although this road is not the same one). '*Iph'indlela,*' he asks, and the answer is contained partly in the very language of the question; the 'road' or way is one that will be coded from the point of view of the question, the question's frame and address already beginning to provide the accented answer.

To return to the seminar room and the tea room at the university where Tlhalo Raditlhalo is suspicious of his colleagues' intentions: there is cause for suspicion and mistrust in institutions that insist on change but speak only in the monolingual voice without imagining the intersections with other languages. Ndebele, like Raditlhalo, insists on the validity of the viewpoint that is at home at the intersection. It is a viewpoint with other premises, rooted in contexts other than the contexts of apartheid, of exclusionary intellectual and political practices, and of the monolingual viewpoint. The viewpoints that it is suspicious of are those often insistent on their own good intentions and their neutrality, on the fact that the work of race (or unracing) is done and we are all, post 1994, equal now.

And this is where Tlhalo Raditlhalo's reading of Ndebele provides an illuminating illustration of Ndebele's own theory of interpretation. Read against the background of a certain tradition, Ndebele's work risks being 'contained'. Read against the background of another tradition, the work's significance is different. To use the logic of Ndebele's argument, a reader should take note of the 'viewpoint' of the work, the intertextual field (which includes reversing traditions of monolingualism) it calls into being. Raditlhalo aims to place Ndebele in a particular tradition of reading and writing, a tradition he clearly wishes to share and develop. His piece performs, ideally, the work my book aims to describe and prescribe. In this version, intertextuality is a way of pointing out fracture and absence, and insisting on the need for mistrust and suspicion. But the road also leads out of that suspicion, towards the mutual vulnerability that Ndebele's work develops and encourages – towards accented thinking.

Chapter 4

THEMBINKOSI GONIWE'S EYES

IN this chapter, the location of accented thinking is once again a university campus. This time the intellectual space is not provided by the tearoom or the staffroom, and the histories of these spaces' referential frameworks and tastes. This chapter analyses two related scenes. The first is a large public artwork displayed on the outside wall of a student residence in Rondebosch, Cape Town. It is a work of art by artist, curator and academic Thembinkosi Goniwe, and it thematises the asymmetrically aligned viewpoints that are the focus of my own book. The artwork is untitled, but is closely associated with the larger public arts project called 'Returning the Gaze', and is sometimes referred to by that title. In its depiction of two faces (white/black) and two kinds of gaze (direct/ averted), it invites an oppositional reading, perhaps *the* reading of South African history: racialised opposites. The second scene I analyse is an academic seminar held at the same university where the artwork was made and exhibited, in a building called 'The African Studies Gallery', entitled 'Insides and Outsides', at which the artist (and subject) of the image, Goniwe, is a speaker.

I want in the discussion here to draw attention to an encounter, a disagreement, that highlights the ways in which ostensibly neutral assumptions and ideas function to keep some referents unreadable. The chapter develops the ideas around resistance and accent, and illustrates the argument through a discussion of staged and performed misunderstanding.

The inside/outside dichotomies have to do, in the first place, with historical inequalities, and with apartheid's ambitions to decree who is inside the learning environment, what knowledge is inside, how teachers and academic institutions regulate what is practised inside, and what is to remain outside (outside the canon, outside the debate, outside the footnotes and bibliographies). The inside/outside dichotomy features as the structuring idea in the account I give of a disagreement, a difference of opinion, between two colleagues at the seminar. In this expression of difference, what is at stake is precisely whose knowledge is 'inside', whose is 'outside'. It is a disagreement that can be interpreted as a failed engagement (a *lack* of communication) that leads to silence. But it can also be interpreted, more positively, as an example of precisely the kinds of disagreements that are needed in this long ending of apartheid we are living through – in other words, an example of meaningful, productive and accented communication. The disagreement attaches itself to footnotes and sources, and to the kinds of intertextual links we bring to the material we view and study. In this part of the analysis, I make the link to my previous chapter's way of understanding intertextuality, as not neutral and natural, but as activist and deliberate. In talking about inside and outside, I show, the disagreement can be understood as bringing to the surface those inequalities and asymmetries that often remain invisible. I aspire, in this book, to make visible some of these invisible asymmetries.

From among a number of possible art projects that provide instances of 'accent' as I have theorised it in the introduction (ways of making explicit an engagement with location, with a particular set of references and intertexts), the one I am most drawn to is the work of art by Thembinkosi Goniwe, part of the 2000 'Returning the Gaze' project. More than perhaps any other South African work of art, this one speaks to me of the orientation of our knowledge and our learning, and the awareness of the relationship between utterance and scene of reception. As it is a work of art that was made for public spaces, the addressee of the work is thus explicitly a general and unspecific one – the public. It was displayed as a banner on the wall of a building that houses students who attend the University of Cape Town. As you walked down the hill from the University of Cape Town campus, you faced it; as you went

Thembinkosi Goniwe, 'Untitled' from the 2000 project 'Returning the gaze'.

Billboard displayed on Main Road, Rondebosch.

towards the university, you had to turn your back on it. It was hung at the intersection of routes: towards and away from, the university.

The work shows the viewer two faces, and it is important to see the two together, to do the obvious and immediate work of comparing them. There are two men. The one on the left does not meet the viewer's gaze. He is dressed in black, his skin is light. The man on the right does meet our gaze. He wears a white shirt with a grey trim around the V-neck, his skin is dark, his eyes haunting. Both men have on their cheeks a plaster, of the kind that is sometimes described as 'skin-coloured'. The implications of this aspect of the work are clear – it is a work that comments on what is regarded as the norm, as normative, the standard against which things (including skin and wounds) have been and perhaps continue to be measured in South Africa. On the light face the plaster is invisible, on the darker skin it is clearly seen. This part of the work is interesting enough, but it is more complex, and more challenging than a mere interrogation of notions of signification and standards (that is, the 'standard' colour of skin, with 'whiteness' taken as the norm).

That the subject on the left looks away is perhaps the most intriguing aspect of the work. Is the subject looking away in shame? Or in embarrassment? Is this a comment on the unwillingness of the subject to engage with the viewer, or with the other figure? What Goniwe wants to represent is not the mutuality of the gaze (*returning* the gaze). He wants to draw attention to the fact that one figure does return the gaze, the other not. The man on the right *is* returning the gaze – of the viewer. But Goniwe means more than this. For him it is important that it is a black subject who returns the gaze, the gaze that has for so long fixed the black subject as that which is gazed at.

The subject on the left does not meet our gaze, and we are forced to look at him precisely *not looking*. The viewer's point of reference is therefore unstable. If you look at the subject on the right, you meet his gaze and see his wound. If your eyes move to the left, you see the subject who refuses to see you – and whose wound is less visible. So, we are made to see him *not see*; that is what the double portrait forces us to look at.

For the viewer whose eyes do not stray from the subject on the right, the 'work' of the double portrait is clear in its political force. There is a wound, there is a historical inequality in terms of objectifying gazes, there is an agent whose gaze challenges this state of affairs. This reading of the artwork does not require the subject on the left to be there; the work is readable in this way as a single portrait. It is interesting to know, but not essential, that the face on the right is a self-portrait of Goniwe, the face on the left one of his teachers (and later, when Goniwe becomes a teacher at the university, one of his colleagues) at the Michaelis School of Art at the University of Cape Town. This reading of the work of art, as a portrait of the relationship between a teacher and a student (and the choices made by the artist encourage us to see this relationship as racialised) makes it powerful in new ways. If we read this as a portrait of the pedagogical situation, the teacher's averted gaze is inflected with looking out of the frame, looking to the left (conventionally seen as looking 'back'). In this reading of the work, the student is 'reversing the gaze' of the teacher-student encounter, talking and teaching back.

This artwork has a curious afterlife, related to the reading of it as a portrait of pedagogical practice. When one searches for the work on the Internet, it now appears in two types of places. Sometimes it is attached to the signature of Goniwe alone, at other times jointly to his signature and that of the man looking away (Malcolm Payne). In one case they are even described as collaborators on the project (O'Toole 2011). This second signature is sometimes described as belonging to Goniwe's 'colleague', at other times his 'teacher'. The extent of the project's collaboration or co-authoring is what is at stake; understood in a different way, it is about who owns what is learned in the classroom.

I want for now to leave aside the afterlives of the work, and the afterlives of the relationship depicted in it. The interpretation I have given of the work puts the emphasis on what is suggested by the title 'Returning the Gaze'. The interlocutor of Goniwe's work of art, it would seem, is assumed to be his *other*, and in particular an other whose motives and interpretation of history he mistrusts and challenges, someone he *knows* does not share his viewpoint and language. Or, at least, this is the position he forces his viewer to adopt, and to feel what it might be like to be so mistrusted. As I argued in the previous chapter, in the discussion of Tlhalo Raditlhalo's performed inability to interpret the tearoom (or his performed inability to be understood by the tearoom), it is not necessary to evaluate whether this mistrust is justified. To defend oneself against the accusing gaze, or to prove one is not implicated in it, is to miss the point of the work, which forces the viewer to adopt and inhabit (resistantly, reluctantly) the position of one who is so mistrusted. The invisibility of the plaster on the face that looks away might also be a comment on the fact that those who cannot 'see' the wound – in themselves, in the communication act, in the dialogue – are the ones who look away. But the wound is there, or at least the trace of the wound, because the plaster is not the wound.

This brings me to the second scene, the seminar on 'Insides and outsides: Race and identity', seen again through Goniwe's eyes. The seminar took place on a Saturday in September 2006, and was organised by Wandile Goozen Kasibe, then an MA student in Fine Arts at the University of Cape Town. The host, Kasibe describes himself poetically, in the introductory remarks to the conference, as 'psychologically homeless, displaced by a language not [my] own and a culture [I have] shrugged on like a coat' (Kasibe 2006). For this Saturday seminar, Kasibe invited a number of scholars on identity and race to present papers, and it is the way that two of these scholars interacted (and did not interact) that is the focus of my discussion, for I find in the disagreement a cluster of words around 'inside' and 'outside', and around 'influence' and 'intertextuality'. The conflict was between Goniwe and a colleague, art historian Liese van der Watt, who was also invited to give a paper. In his introductory remarks Kasibe (2006) says:

> At this critical time in our history we need a discourse that will com-
> fort and discomfort, the one that has potency to hurt and heal at the
> same time. Our discourse should encourage social and academic cohe-
> sion and shun racial schisms so that we may look at one another not
> as different entities but as entities deliberately brought together by the
> forces of history from which we cannot isolate ourselves. We all carry
> one another's scars.

The reference to scars, to our eyes now used to seeing the plasters on Goniwe's art work, inserts a possible interpretive position. Are we meant to read Goniwe's work as a work about the mutual, shared carrying of scars? Is what is at stake the acknowledgement that all bodies, all South Africans, are united in the scarred history we share? Or is this sharing more along the lines of what Njabulo Ndebele (2007: 137) writes about when he says:

> We are all familiar with the global sanctity of the white body. Wher-
> ever the white body is violated in the world, severe retribution follows
> somehow for the perpetrators if they are non-white, regardless of the
> social status of the white body. The white body is inviolable, and that
> inviolability is in direct proportion to the global vulnerability of the
> black body. This leads me to think that if South African whiteness is a
> beneficiary of the protectiveness assured by international whiteness, it
> has an opportunity to write a new chapter in world history. It will have

to come out from under the umbrella and repudiate it. Putting itself at risk, it will have to declare that it is home now, sharing in the vulnerability of other compatriots bodies. South African whiteness will declare that its dignity is inseparable from the dignity of black bodies.

If we think of sharing in this sense, it is a sharing that – instead of declaring the share equal, balanced, mutual – is a way of drawing attention precisely to the *lack* of mutuality. When Goniwe places a plaster on each of the faces of his subjects, the visual impression made by the two plasters is very different. In his opening remarks, Kasibe devotes considerable time to the topic of 'whiteness studies'. His remarks introduce works that pose a challenge:

> ... to all of us in our different areas of specialisation to reason consciously as to why is there a lack of scrutiny on 'whiteness'. Is it because 'whiteness' is still perceived as the standard by which other bodies are measured? Why is the subject of 'whiteness' still on the margins of our collegial discourses? Is there perhaps a conspiracy? Why is the black subject always an easy target of scrutiny when there is a problematic 'white' subject that has not been widely exposed? ... My concern is in the slow speed at which this critique is moving, particularly in a country that is still trying to come to terms with its own self. As we reason about and digest these questions, the aim should not be to formulate any stricture or discourse against 'white' bodies but to problematise what has for many centuries been regarded as the norm and standard, if you will.

Kasibe's introduction aims to distinguish whiteness as the colour of skin from whiteness as the colour of what he calls 'consciousness'. His comments invite the participants to 'argue across their own territorial, spatial and racial limitations', and he expresses a wish that the seminar's participants will 'aim to understand and embrace one another'. In the spirit of this vision (sharing the wounds, transcending limitations), the participants are invited to give their papers.

Liese van der Watt, one of the invited speakers and at the time a lecturer at the university, had presented a paper on a topic related to her PhD work, on what she called 'exiting whiteness'. Her work is influenced by the theoretical work on whiteness studies in the United States, where she studied, and where she graduated with a PhD from the State University of New York. This work is the very same work that has been mentioned by

Kasibe, and it seems still that there is a shared vision of the seminar. Van der Watt brings to her work a South African inflection – in particular she wants to mobilise 'exiting whiteness' in the service of a nonracial future where race does not figure in any of the apartheid senses of the word. Her paper assumes that there will be sympathy between her and Goniwe (Kasibe's introduction has confirmed this sense that work on whiteness is valuable, and that it has a place in the academy), that their theoretical positions are compatible, and that their political ideals will rhyme. In Goniwe's reading of her paper, and an earlier paper, to which he also refers, and in particular in her theorisation of what is termed 'post-race', there is on the contrary a display (a performance) of a breakdown in communication, and a breakdown of comprehension. Instead of Goniwe listening to and responding to this work as 'shared', he instead chooses to emphasise metaphors of inside/outside, to show where he and van der Watt disagree, where they do *not* share.

There are ways of interpreting this exchange – or lack of exchange – that can lead one to positions of silence and passivity; the lesson one could take from this exchange is that the time for certain academics, for certain South Africans, is 'over' (exit whites, rather than exit whiteness). It is a common enough discourse. I want to understand this disagreement, instead, as an example of the kinds of difficult and challenging engagements of which we need more. In other words, instead of seeing this disagreement as a failure to communicate, I want to read it for what it can reveal to us, and what we can learn from this seeming failure. The instance of demonstrated non-communication is in fact a very successful form of communication, even an ideal form of understanding. And the understanding is one that wants to insist on non-equivalence, on difference, on inside/outside; it is accented. What Goniwe intends to demonstrate with this performance of disagreement, is that the transformation of South African society is incomplete – or in the words of my own Introduction, we are still living through the long ending of apartheid.

In his conference paper, 'Negotiating space: Some matters in South African contemporary art' Goniwe (2006: 1) writes (or says, since we ought in this argument to imagine the room, to reconstruct the context, and the atmosphere of the interactions):

> Blacks remain restrained to move as freely, control their movements, cultivate and nurture their personal, family, communal, social and cultural practices as whites do. As such, blacks are not primarily (*for*)

themselves in South Africa; their being and becoming are subject to socio-economic conditions dictated by whites, albeit in a world governed by black politicians.

Goniwe's argument continues, built up often around metaphors of inside/ outside, inclusion/exclusion. In a footnote, for example, he writes (2006: 14, n5):

> These are theories and discussions [about identity politics] that have been initiated around the world, and beginning outside of South Africa. Their regurgitation and application in South African context insinuates an agenda by a larger group of white South African critics/ art historians specifically, from a single reference, attributed to other international theorists, by Liese van der Watt in an exhibition catalogue for the exhibition 'Personal Affects' which looked specifically at the problematic of defining identity in contemporary art.

Footnotes, of course, are often the trail that can lead us to that on which an argument is built; and in this case the footnotes show not only on what ground Goniwe wishes to build, but also – and in particular – on what he does *not* want to build his argument. His insistence on inside/ outside, on space as his structuring device, makes it clear that he wants to keep some ideas, some assumptions *outside* of his own argument. He wants to claim what he calls the 'space'. It is the verbal equivalent of returning the gaze, of claiming a particular kind of agency and pointing out how this agency has historically been shaped. The title of the paper uses the word 'negotiate', but Goniwe does not demonstrate that conciliatory tone (it is a tone present in Kasibe's introduction, but not in Goniwe's paper). Instead, his opening reference to the 1913 and 1936 Land Acts makes clear that he is thinking in terms of (re?)claiming rather than negotiating, and this becomes even clearer later in the piece. Revealing is also the term 'regurgitation', a word that implies that the ideas to which he refers have not been absorbed, not been placed, in his view, *inside*, can be brought in and taken out again without changing the words and ideas around them. In other words, what he finds in van der Watt's work is an example of ideas that do *not* activate what are, for him, the appropriate intertextual referents.

When one reads the companion piece by Liese van der Watt, ('Personal affects: Power and poetics in contemporary South African art'), the ideas that Goniwe wants to keep *outside* are revealed to be her thoughts around understandings of the term 'post'. For Goniwe this argument is 'problematic' (inappropriate, needs to be kept outside) because it 'confuses blacks protesting against the circumstances that dictate what it means to be black, rather than what it is to be black'. The distinction Goniwe makes here is thus between 'being' and 'meaning'; his argument wants to hold on to the fact that 'what it means to be black' is not essentialist, but that blackness is a way of inhabiting a position the very existence of which has been ignored. His argument then develops an anti-essentialist strand, which in a sense rhymes with van der Watt's argument. But then he comes to the crux of his disagreement with her: 'What is questionable is the *timing* of van der Watt's call for post-identity. It pops up when black subjects are just beginning to gain visibility, recognition and significance – personal liberties which colonial and apartheid regimes officially condemned, repressed, even erased' (2006: 2). So, Goniwe argues, the struggle has been 'to gain grounds to make *visible*, and thus recognisable and valid, that which their white oppressors rendered invisible and invalid'.

It is in the interpretation of a particular artwork that Goniwe finds the illustration of his claim to a difference of 'ground' from van der Watt. The artwork is a video installation by Churchill Madikida, called *Struggles of the Heart*. In the video, the artist is seen eating and spitting out mielie pap – regurgitating, one might say. Goniwe's reading of the installation is informed by Madikida's 'situatedness', the dense web of contextual and cultural associations evoked by the installation. Van der Watt's reading of the video, in Goniwe's words, is 'unblinking', again a bodily metaphor, and a metaphor about the nature of the gaze. What he is saying is that there is a work of art which performs and uses the body in a way that particular knowledge systems, historically determined, allow him to 'see', and that van der Watt does not 'see'. She 'sees' something which is (too?) quick (a way of looking that is the blink of an eye), her interaction with the work of art is informed by her theories acquired 'outside', which she 'insinuates' into a debate where it cannot (or has not) been absorbed and which hence seem like regurgitation. The description of a gaze as 'unblinking' is hard to read – an unblinking look may be interpreted as defiant, challenging, and perhaps unreflective. What Goniwe means is more closely related to not seeing than seeing too much; the too-open eyes are meant to denote not insight, but a form of not-seeing. The position Goniwe describes has a visual equivalent – the image of Malcolm Payne not looking, not reversing the viewer's gaze.

Goniwe's response to van der Watt is to question, and to find wanting, the intertextual field she activates in her reading. When we read his text, images of ground, property, land and territory build up a dense metaphoric field. He calls the paper 'negotiating space' (a much-used term in South African discourse at the time), and here it is perhaps productive to read the word 'negotiating' as a qualifier of space, an adjective of the kind of space Goniwe wants to create in and for his work. Both papers are influenced by the debates around representation (both writers are well-read, have read similar theories, have received a similar university education, have studied in the USA, have international degrees), but Goniwe wants the theory to be 'accented' in a particularly South African way. He wants to look not at their commonality, but at their difference. It is worth pointing out that Goniwe is thinking structurally about race, privilege and point of view. In a now rather famous open letter which became known as 'Targeted Candidate' written to the South African National Gallery in response to the wording of a job advertisement, Goniwe (2006) asked:

> Please consider my concerns regarding your advertised Trainee Curator at the SANG. I am wondering how many potential candidates 'from historically disadvantaged groups' that would apply given the stipulated required 'Minimum qualification: BA Degree in Fine Arts or History of Art'. I am thinking of young black art practitioners who have no university or college qualification as required, for example graduates from Community Art Projects (now Arts and Media Access Centre), Ruth Prowse, FUNDA, etc – from community driven initiatives or organisations! The question then, who really is your targeted candidate 'from historically disadvantaged groups', if those without formally recognised qualifications seem to be calculatedly excluded regarding unaddressed politics of 'qualification'? Maybe this recruitment should be clear about its targeted candidate. Be frank about inviting or soliciting formally trained (university/college) graduates. If that being the case, then remove such patronising stigma: 'historically disadvantaged groups'! For some black students with university/college degrees in Fine Arts are not from disadvantaged families; some are from middle and upper class families who do not neatly and unproblematically fit into the categorisation: 'historically disadvantaged groups'.

This letter was written in July 2006, a few months before the 'Race and identity' seminar. It shows Goniwe questioning the language of the advertisement and revealing the invisible assumptions behind it. The advertisement is inviting black candidates to apply ('targeting' them, in Goniwe's words). Goniwe wants to point out not only the history of the institution and how it is implicated in a racialised understanding of qualifications, but also that it is not enough to make a seemingly open invitation, when the terms of the invitation clearly limit who might successfully respond to ' ,e invitation. There are echoes of Njabulo Ndebele's address to the English Academy of South Africa, discussed in the previous chapter.

Kasibe's and Goniwe's work share a point of view, and at times some terminology, with Okwui Enwezor's influential paper 'Reframing the black subject: Ideology and fantasy in contemporary South African representation', published originally in 1997 and republished in 1999 in *Reading the Contemporary*, in which Enwezor (1997:377) takes issue with white South African artists' representations of what he calls, using the singular form, 'the black subject'. Enwezor argues that whites have for too long been the framers, and blacks those who are framed. His piece is not concerned so much with theorising the reframing of the black subject (and, for that matter, the white subject) as seen through black eyes. Instead he provides an analysis of some recent works by white South African artists, artists who are the white interlocutors and interpreters of symbolic and literal images of the black body, those 'highly literate, but nonetheless unreflexive white cultural practitioners unblinkingly intent on representing black subjectivity at the margins of cultural and aesthetic discourse' (1997: 384-5).

Enwezor's argument aims, through analysing a number of examples, to prove how white artists and theorists find (that is, in his argument, *misrepresent*) black subjectivity as being in the margins; but also how these representations aim to (and often succeed in) keeping black subjectivity at the margins. Enwezor's subject (similar to the subject of Goniwe's artwork, and the subject constructed in Goniwe's reading of van der Watt) is described as 'unblinking'. The 'unblinking' subject is the subject who assumes we all have the same 'regime of looking' (1997: 393). In his reading of van der Watt, Goniwe provides examples of intertexts he activates automatically, and she (or someone like her) does not; and I want to look at how it is he explains this, if it is not 'race', as he is at pains to argue. Elsewhere in his paper Enwezor writes of 'ethical blinkers familiar to all redemptive colonial errands' (1997: 393). Whereas blinkers prevent a certain kind of sight, unblinking has a different, more challenging connotation. The unblinking gaze is perhaps closer to the imagined interlocutor of Ndebele's work, or Raditlhalo's staff seminar. Even if the subject believes herself not to be on a colonial errand, this theoretical version goes, she needs to imagine what it would be like, what the consequences are, for the gaze that positions her there. In other words, even when (maybe particularly when) she believes herself not to be on a colonial errand, she has to imagine the positions of those who could interpret her works as such. That a reader of this book will find the work also in pursuit of a colonial, self-forgiving errand, is one of the positions I have had to incorporate in my thinking.

Goniwe is claiming not that he sees the work of art more clearly because he is black, but that he brings to his viewing a different set of knowledges and contextualising systems. In another footnote, he quotes from Linda Martin Alcoff's *Visible Identities: Race, Gender, and the Self*: 'When I refuse to listen to how you are different from me, I refuse to know who you are. But without understanding fully who you are, I will never be able to appreciate precisely how we are more alike than I might have originally supposed' (quoted in Goniwe, n15). Alcoff's argument is attached here to support Goniwe's argument about inside/outside: in order to agree (or to see how we are similar – as these two writers' arguments often are), it is crucial that we/you need to acknowledge at the outset how we/you are differently positioned. And so, Goniwe's argument seems to go, there can be no inside before we acknowledge that there has been/is an outside. Goniwe's 'outside' is the outside of 'apart-heid' (as he spells it, underlining the sense of outside/inside), and he needs to have it acknowledged that he has been outside the 'space'. The other 'outside', the 'regurgitated theory', is theory that is not sensitive enough to its (that is, his) context. Looked at in a certain way, van der Watt's theories rhyme with Goniwe's. But Goniwe wants to assert that it is in her use of the theory, in her 'outside' use, that she does not sufficiently acknowledge the difference of his opinion.

Goniwe's argument turns here to the trope I have been waiting for: translation. He discusses a 2002 work, *(un)hea(r)d*, by Thando Mama, a video installation. Goniwe's argument is made through how he sees the work. In this work, he writes, Mama's 'portrait takes up the entire screen monitor, while whispering sounds in code-switch between English and Xhosa augment the force of the projection' (2006: 5). Goniwe's reading of this work is that 'sound questions language as a medium of communication and carrier of culture, especially its defining, dividing, repressive and exclusionary mechanisms'. He continues: 'Mama reflects on the continuing situatedness of the racialised black subject in society, challenging the pretentious ideals of liberalism or democracy that remain complacent to particularised experiences of black people.' His viewing is influenced by Ngũgĩ wa Thiong'o's interest in 'colonial alienation', developed in *Decolonising the Mind*, which 'would mean the black African must not only "stand outside of himself to look at himself", he must also embody a split persona: "like separating the mind from the body so that they are occupying two unrelated linguistic spheres in the same person"' (quoted in Goniwe 2006: 5).

What Goniwe takes issue with is not necessarily van der Watt's theory – after all, this is the kind of theory that the seminar host encouraged and welcomed. He is at pains to show that even when he and van der Watt use the same or similar theoretical readings as the basis of their work, their relationship to this scholarship is asymmetrical – informed by their history, and so not the same. For Kasibe to speak of whiteness is an example of returning the gaze; for me, it is not and cannot be. This is perhaps one of the pitfalls of whiteness studies – it risks perpetuating an interest in whiteness, in particular when the work is done by scholars who, as South Africans understand immediately even when we reject these classifications, are white. Even when it wants to make whiteness visible, and interrogate whiteness as normative, the attention to whiteness perpetuates the sense of its importance. Enwezor pointed, in his 1997 paper, to a strand in discourses of whiteness (discourses that are in their own eyes aligned to the post-apartheid project – clearly racist uses of whiteness function differently) that searched for the erasure of conflict and accountability. 'Apartheid is dead', and therefore whiteness has been cleansed, so this fallacy goes.

Goniwe turns from whiteness, invoking instead the classical reference of Ngũgĩ wa Thiong'o's understanding of the black subject. Goniwe's reading of Mama alongside Ngũgĩ reflects on 'the African's' relationship to languages and multilingual situations. Mama's work, Goniwe remarks, 'asks how South Africans can understand each other if language remains a racial factor', in other words if some viewers can experience the work's soundtrack as partly unintelligible. So the viewer may think she understands (in the blink of an eye) the work's significance; but if she cannot bring to the soundtrack a particular kind of linguistic knowledge, the work remains self-consciously impenetrable (leaves her 'outside' the signification systems). Mama, in Goniwe's reading, does this deliberately, in order to:

> ... illuminate the fact that the transforming subject is mainly black: speaking English for blacks is about accessing whites; enabling

communication within spheres that are favourable to whites. Yet, how can whites *hear* blacks in their fractured grammar, obscure and reinvented English language? Can blacks speak in the colonial or master language in ways that will produce a shift towards inequality and justice in society? Are whites listening, let alone able to hear what blacks are saying? Who is Mama's black subject speaking to, 'unhearing' and afraid of? (2006: 5).

The sentence contorts, and the reader is left uncertain who is afraid – is it Mama expressing fear through his whispers (the English whispers), or is it the Xhosa-language whispers that express fear, or instil fear? It does not matter much which way one reads it, since Goniwe's argument wants to work in both ways, showing how ignorant 'outside' eyes and ears are built into, and in fact constitute, the meaning of the work.

What Goniwe wants, he shows, is an art-critical practice that does the work of 'working through', of the 'dramatic process of transformation, undoing of colonialism and apartheid consequences'. His work wants to insist that there are no easy ways of arriving at a 'post' (post-apartheid, post-colonialism, post-race) position, but that there is work to be done towards that point. His evocative 2000 artwork still resonates, directing the gaze backwards, forwards, from side to side. The aim is to force the reader to inhabit a series of positions, and thereby to reposition (and be repositioned; and to be positioned exactly there where self-forgiving discourses make it uncomfortable to be). So every interpreting act, any communicating act, has the potential to shift the weight of where the encoding and decoding take place.

I do not wish to underplay the affect and conflict of this encounter, but in this difference of opinion, and the theorisation around what you can see – depending on your point of view and what theoretical machinery you bring to the viewing – there is a clear instance of what accented discourse could look and sound like. In this disagreement, and the insistence on difference, I see the way towards the ending of apartheid and its discourses. Kasibe's welcoming speech mentions discourses that 'comfort and discomfort', the implication being that to communicate means to acknowledge that tension and difference is inevitable. An accented tradition will inevitably acknowledge that South Africans are tied together by a shared destiny, and what we share is exactly the legacy of our differences.

A theme that runs through Goniwe's paper, Enwezor's argument, and some of Ndebele's work, is that of the communicative act which is decoded in ways that bring the very act into question or under suspicion. Such a communicative act activates intertexts that cast doubt over the explicitly stated force of the communicative act, and the listener or hearer detects a disjunction between the communication and the context, or between the address and the assumptions underlying it. So, in my reading, Goniwe is *staging* a misunderstanding in order to make his point about black subjects being misunderstood and misrepresented. I do not mean by this that he is falsifying, rather that his words carry the intended meaning and *in addition* perform that very meaning.

In JL Austin's *How to do Things with Words* he makes a distinction between the phrases 'I am running' and 'I apologise':

> We might say: in ordinary cases, for example running, it is the fact that he is running which makes the statement that he is running *true*; or, again, that the truth of the constative utterance 'he is running' depends on his being running. Whereas in our case it is the happiness of the performative 'I apologise' which makes it the fact that I am apologising: and my success in apologising depends on the happiness of the performative utterance 'I apologise' (1986: 47).

Austin distinguishes performatives from what he calls 'purely polite conventional ritual phrases', which do not have to satisfy a sincerity requirement (1986: 84). This distinction seems to me useful in understanding much of the distrust one finds in some interactions in South African discourse, and some of the disquiet around the public apologies and demands for 'reconciliation' that formed part of the TRC hearings. It is not enough to state 'apartheid is dead', it is not a statement that functions as a performative in Austin's terms. Instead we see, following Goniwe's logic, that the statement may in fact be counter-performative, erasing the work that needs to be done.

Where white critics and artists represent black subjectivity, Enwezor (1999: 393) finds 'unreflexive', 'unblinking' eyes and a voice which addresses the self-same, assumes the self-same to be the standard. Crucial in this mistrust is the audience addressed in the artworks (or exhibitions, or writing). He uses the phrase 'redemptive colonial errands' for the vision of their work some of these whites have: a nostalgia for empire, which is combined with a desire to redeem whiteness. This is the kind of endeavour that is mistrusted by Ndebele, Enwezor and Goniwe. What all three want to direct our gaze at is the kind of thinking that assumes that 'as spectators, we all see the same thing, and thus believe that our gazes are constituted and therefore affirmed and defined by the same regime of looking' (Enwezor 1999: 393). So, for Enwezor, ultimately, the problem with much of the art and academic discourses he analyses, is the 'lack … and non-recognition of the place of the black spectator as an affirmed and enabled participant in the act of looking'.

The 'place' of the black spectator is, in other words, one that needs to be imagined, recognised, learned; and its absences in art and academic discourses need to be theorised and countered. In order to theorise this place, my book has suggested that accented thinking is what can be learned and developed. In confronting the artwork that goes under the title 'Returning the Gaze', every viewer is encouraged, even forced, to remember the histories of the body, and to occupy (even while resisting it) the position of one who looks away, unwilling to meet the gaze. My argument does not advocate that 'I' adopt or pretend to adopt the position of the black spectator. The work in this book is not particularly interested in questions of identity in that sense but, rather, in knowledge and attitudes. What this book strives to do is to argue for the acquisition of knowledge (not necessarily experience) of the referential fields, the language codes and the histories that can inform understandings of not only the artwork, but also the response of others to the artwork. We cannot lay claim to experiences and histories in our scholarship; but there is much work to do to develop ears and eyes attuned to accented knowledge.

Chapter 5

A HISTORY OF TRANSLATION
AND NON-TRANSLATION

THIS chapter develops further the sceptical and uncelebratory under-standings of translation introduced earlier. The histories of translation in early colonial South Africa might have provided an instance of accented interaction, yet did not. Despite the multilingualism of the early encounters, and the presence of a number of skilled translator and interpreter figures, these early instances of translation practices provide us in fact with a clear example of *lack* of accentedness, and *lack* of intertextuality. Instead of the mutuality and equality promised by translation encounters, we find instead examples of unequal language contact, and asymmetries which have remained as dominant features of the South African multi-lingual landscape. This chapter seeks to demythologise translation as a metaphor for greater understanding and identification, and to draw attention to translation's silencing effects. Turning the gaze to this scene of early European settlement seems like acceptance of exactly the vision of South Africa that this project wants to resist, with its assumptions that a European presence, and speakers and writers of European languages, are what make history begin. As Harry Garuba recently put it in a public address at the University of Stellenbosch, 'How *not* to think Africa from the Cape' is the challenge our scholarship needs to set itself. This chapter takes the insights of Ndebele's work about the need to live at the intersection of languages to see how and why the early colonial phase in South African history precisely did not create an intersection of languages despite multilingualism and the multiple acts of translation and interpreting. The interest in this chapter is in multilingualism and the ways in which multilingual environments are not a simple guarantee that accented thinking will necessarily take place.

Although the early colonial encounter (and in particular language contact) is what is at issue, the chapter is constantly on the lookout for ways of avoiding a version of history that privileges the colonial archive. Written documents of early multilingual encounters on South African soil make it obvious that Africa was multilingual long before European ears arrived to hear it. Attempting an accented reading of the written texts of the 'early Cape', this chapter questions closely understandings of multilingualism during the early years of colonial settlement. In particular the argument here is suspicious of readings that want to excavate this multilingualism as evidence of reciprocity and mutuality – as a horizontal contact zone. The thinking in this chapter is to develop a practice of teaching and scholarship that is attuned to its own desire to find (to construct) an idealised and forgiving moment of origin. Conflict and difference, non-understanding and resistance (rather than origin and unity), are what such an accented reading and teaching practice brings to our approaches to this period of South African history.

In analysing these histories of translation and interpreting, I want to place the early written tradition (the documents of European explorers and administrators) next to and against a writing tradition that is earlier than, but also exists contemporarily to, the colonial record: the written tradition represented by the diverse rock engravings and scratchings that are found in South Africa. I am not the first to mention this idea – or, true to this chapter's interests, I am not the 'origin' of it. In her foreword to *Written Culture in a Colonial Context: Africa and the Americas 1500-1900*, Isabel Hofmeyr (2011: x) writes that 'in the southern African historiography it is striking that studies of rock art are seldom brought together with studies of the social history of writing'. Ntongela Masilela, in 'Issues in the historiography of South African literature' writes:

> A historically more plausible location of our writerly literary origins is in the writings or 'scribblings' in Khoikhoi-San cave paintings. ...

[T]he effect of locating our writerly literary origins in these writings would be to extend and expand the longitudinal plane of our literary origins; and this would have the simultaneous effect of deepening the conceptual structure of our literary history (Masilela n.d.).

In this chapter and in the next I link these two early writing traditions (alphabetic European, non-alphabetic African), paying attention to questions of audience and the ways in which these writings circulated, did not circulate, and circulate now in scholarship. In this way, I am trying to see what can be learned if one approaches these early and diverse written documents as the beginnings of a South African literary tradition in which the familiar violent lack of mutual knowledge is implicit. And since I am on the lookout for classrooms and teachers, I also try to understand early language encounters to see how, and to whose benefit, teaching occurs in the encounters where these early texts circulate (and, more significantly, how and why they do *not* circulate).

In this argument I am reacting to an understanding of translation as necessarily benevolent (an attractive approach in many ways, and developed with great sensitivity in Antjie Krog's *A Change of Tongue*, for example), and I caution that our work has histories that are implicated in silencing. We should not be too quick in congratulating ourselves that our scholarship has rescued those traditions and texts that have been obliterated. I return to this question in the next chapter, and the two chapters can be read as a pair – the one interested in the lack of intertextuality inherent in the early colonial encounter, the next more concerned with the ways in which the contemporary scholar comes to take ownership of these traditions, thereby achieving another instance of obliteration.

I begin the discussion by looking at a rather insignificant pamphlet from about a hundred years ago, written by a museum director and addressing an audience with a particular set of expectations about what constitutes history. It is a little pamphlet to document and catalogue a tradition of rock inscription in South Africa. More significant for the context in which I place it here is how it manages to *edit out* a much more obvious and much larger set of rock markings. The pamphlet focuses exclusively on markings left by Europeans on the land, ignoring any marks left by local writers and inscribers. It is an example of an almost wilful lack of intertextuality. Significantly, this pamphlet is published in 1913 – to anyone with a passing knowledge of South African history this year resonates as the year of the Natives' Land Act, which divested Africans of the right to land ownership in all but seven per cent of the country. Thus the publication date confirms the erasure of a pre-European presence and claim to the land, and in its inability to consider rock markings by passing Europeans intertextually alongside other markings it mirrors the agenda of the Land Act.

This pamphlet appeared as a slim volume by the then director of the South African Museum in Cape Town, Louis Albert Péringuey, and is called *Inscriptions Left by Early European Navigators on their Way to the East*. Péringuey was an entomologist and insect taxonomist by profession, and he also appears as a character in the annals of craniometry in South Africa. Patricia Davison, in her foreword to the *Miscast: Negotiating the Presence of the Bushman* catalogue, writes:

> Louis Péringuey, director of the South African Museum from 1906 to 1924, was responsible for assembling a large collection of crania, which he sent to London for morphological analysis, in the hope of characterising physical differences between 'Bush', and 'Khoikhoi', people. After detailed craniometrical study, it was concluded that no morphological distinction could be made.

Péringuey is responsible for initiating the making of life-casts of 'pure-bred Bushmen and Hottentots', a project that has had a vexed afterlife. 'The motivation,' writes Davison of Péringuey's project, was 'a combination of science and salvage' (1996: 11). The salvage work is, however, not intended to save the cultural and social life of these human beings (in contrast then to the aim of the salvage work of a very different tradition in the *Inscriptions* pamphlet), but of their physical form – the way they could be classified in a taxonomy. One can see why an approach such as Péringuey's might lead one to ignoring the written traditions of these men and women and to writing a taxonomy of rock markings that includes only those made by European hands. It is also evident that the audience for the salvation, to whose benefit things or people are 'saved', is crucial in understanding the work.

The booklet was still in print in 1950, in a third edition. It aims to provide a complete 'taxonomy' of early marks left on the country by European travellers, and is fascinating in its assumptions about 'ancient history' in South Africa. 'In a country occupied permanently as recently as 1652, relics of very ancient history cannot be plentiful,' writes Péringuey. The prehistory that he wants to document can be traced 'as far back as 1485', and 'these forerunners of the present Colonists have left a few relics which are the more precious because of their rarity'

(1950: 1). In this version of South African ancient history, the first (the original) markings are those left by the very first Europeans to step onto land from their passing ships. Whatever marks were there before are not regarded as 'relics'. Presumably they form part of another taxonomic system altogether, and are parts of a tradition that cannot be included in the history he writes. Imagining history like this is an aggressive act of willed lack of intertextuality, and the continued effects of this lack of intertextuality linger in our institutions of higher learning.

Péringuey provides a catalogue of the commemorative pillars, inscriptions and stone carvings left by fleets, starting with the landings of Bartholomew Diaz, the first documented European to round the Cape, in 1487. During this time (historicised in a particular way as the reign of King Juan the Second of Portugal), 'discoverers were, for the first time, provided with commemorative pillars, *padrões*, to be erected at the farthest point reached, or to mark the progress of their journey' (1950: 4). A fragment of one of possibly five crosses planted by Diaz, writes Péringuey, is exhibited in the museum (which no longer exists). This cross, which marks the first landing by a European ship, he continues, 'was originally erected on the summit of a small granite eminence, and was discovered by Captain Owen in 1833, but [quoting Owen] "cast down evidently by design as the part of the shaft that had originally been buried in the rock had remained unbroken".' Interesting in this scene of secondary discovery is the re-enactment of the first, the 'original', landing. The discovery of the first landing seems to validate this as the scene of origin, but there is also evidence that the marker of this origin has been tampered with, that these markings and what they represent are vulnerable to being forgotten. In other words, Péringuey manages to create for the reader a scene of discovery which enacts the fragility and the threats to this site. The looming danger is the unmentioned, deliberately unnoticed local inhabitants – about whom the text cannot speak while insisting on primacy.

Following the crosses, the taxonomy moves on to one of the more strangely memorable scenes from this early colonial history, the leaving of a letter in a shoe, in some accounts a shoe left hanging from a tree. The shoe in this origin myth was found by a later passing ship's captain, who in his turn left an engraved stone of which only a fragment remains. So a shoe is left containing a letter, and the shoe is in turn replaced with a stone including a fragment of a text. The atmosphere of this anecdote is dense with loss and the threat of loss. The inscription, writes Péringuey, is 'very baffling owing to its present incompleteness' (1950: 7). Images of decay and wreckage multiply, as evidence of the 'ancient' origins of these objects, and also as a chronicle of heroism against forces of destruction (human and natural). The taxonomy continues, describing and sometimes providing photographs of various stone fragments, in what wants to be a complete taxonomy of these heroic remains.

Noticeable in this account is the absence of human interaction. The engravings seem to be left on a timeless and deserted landscape; the markings and the documents of their discovery create an intertextual web of references that manages not to engage with anyone who is not 'on their way' elsewhere, as the title of the pamphlet indicates. It is in the section entitled 'Post Office Stones' that the first references are made to 'the natives'. Péringuey's account stresses, and in fact his argument relies on, the fact that the landscape lacks 'very ancient relics' before the erection and construction of the European crosses and stones. But once there is an acknowledgement of the presence of local inhabitants, his narrative of lack and absence begins to strain. Introducing the idea of a post office (a term that recurs in histories of this period) provides a role for local inhabitants – as guardians and custodians (but not ever producers or consumers) of the early historical record.

Péringuey (himself French-born, although here it is not relevant other than to know that his French was fluent, and perhaps to remember that he too was in some degree transient in South Africa), quotes from the ship's log of a French commander Beaulieu, who was on a voyage to Bantam via Senegal and the Gold Coast where he traded (1950: 12), and who landed in Table Bay on 16 March 1620:

> Some of our men going ashore happened to light upon a great stone, with two little packets of pitched canvas underneath, which we afterwards found to be Dutch letters. When we opened them we found first a strong piece of pitched canvas, then a piece of lead wrapped round the packet; under that two pieces of red cloth, then a piece of red frieze, all wrapped round a bag of coarse linen in which were the letters very safe and dry. They contained an account of several ships that had passed that way; particularly of an English advice boat that was gone to England to acquaint the Company with the injury the Dutch had done them in the East Indies. They likewise gave notice to ships that passed that way to take care of the natives who had murdered several of their crew, and stole some of their water-casks (quoted in Péringuey 1950: 12).

We read in this archive of how the documents were wrapped in layers to preserve them – in oil-cloth, sail, sometimes even in lead. Of course the purpose was to preserve these letters until they could be read by their intended readers; but there is also an acknowledgement of the urge to protect against the locality and weather conditions.

Clear from this account is the paranoid relationship between Dutch and English ships, and the hostility and competition between the Dutch East India Company and the British East India Company. There is a substantial literature on the intense competition between rival trade companies and empires, and the resulting need for secrecy (see for example Leibbrandt, 1906: 56, 58, 102). In the very familiar version of origins (one I resist, but which needs to be invoked for the reader who may not immediately recognise the date as significant), the Dutch East India Company (the VOC), a trading company with profit as its main aim, established the Cape as a refreshment station for ships on their way to the east in 1652, and made it compulsory for all its ships to stop over at the Cape. The Company required of its commanders to keep meticulous accounts and to write journals and reports that were regularly despatched, in multiple sealed copies, to offices in Batavia and in the Netherlands. These accounts were regarded as secret, for the eyes of the Company only; trade routes and information about potentially profitable ventures were guarded, and sometimes even written in code. Significantly, then, the intended audience of writing at the early Cape often (even typically) excluded those actually living at the Cape. This point is worth stressing. While VOC culture was highly literate, and invested in writing and documentation, it was also a tradition that did not allow this written knowledge to circulate. It is an extreme version of a system of knowledge that does not imagine or allow the knowledge to be shared, in the interest of profit and protection of internal gains and privileges.

Interesting in the letter quoted by Péringuey, the English translation of which uses the word 'likewise', is the parallel set up between dangers posed by rival commercial trading companies and the danger posed by 'the natives'. The French commander continues his narrative, referring to 'one of the natives that spoke a sort of jargon of broken English [and who] gave us to understand more by signs than by his language that five ships had sailed from thence to the eastward about three months before' (1950: 13). The 'native' addresses the French captain in 'a jargon of broken English', but the record remains silent on the commander's own English (of course reading this in English translation dilutes the sense of the French captain's own possibly tenuous relationship to English). Then the report shifts in its description of the speaker of broken English, as his language is said to disappear entirely and the 'native' speaks 'more by signs than by his language' of violence. It is not clear why the speaker uses sign language; one possibility of course is the limited comprehension he finds in his listeners, the French captain and his crew. What I want to underline here, though, is the discourse of incomprehensibility (rather than a discourse of incomprehension and lack of knowledge on the part of the French crew) that attaches itself to the 'natives', a topic to which my argument returns.

In Péringuey's understanding, the European ships arrive in a world where language is almost absent, and the markings left on the landscape by the European ships are prefigurings of a later heroic settlement. In the work of historians of this obsessively well-documented and analysed period, historians such as R Raven Hart and CR Boxer, we see these same tropes repeated, the narrative of the early encounter based around ships' documents and their engravings on the land. The postal system (letters under rocks and markings engraved on rocks) is read in this literature for what it reveals of those who travelled here in search of trade routes and profit. In recent work on the Dutch East India Empire, this approach to landing places as sites in a larger empire of knowledge is highlighted, broadening our understanding of networks of knowledge (for a useful overview see Worden 2007). Yet this scholarship also confirms the lack of intertextual engagement with local people and their knowledge systems. The letters are part of closed circuits of readership. Not only are transit and travel the theme, but the letters themselves create a discourse of unsettledness and of profit accruing somewhere else (in the company offices in Amsterdam).

By looking here at what is called the 'early Cape' (Cape Town as Mother City, with all the connotations of origin and primacy) I do not mean to repeat this version of South African history and writing traditions. In fact, I would prefer not to rehearse once again the background and viewpoints of this extremely familiar (*to some*, and not to others, and that is the main point) history. Instead, my interest is in what we can learn from how this material has been read and misread. In Chapter 9 I consider what the referents and histories are that we have in the classroom or the library, and which referents and intertextual webs of knowledge are not there. It is a way of thinking about choices and syllabuses, of course, but it is also an attempt at thinking about the histories and pre-histories of written traditions in South Africa.

Thinking about which texts we read in the classroom, and which texts we want our students to know, we also need to consider the absence of texts, and how they have come to be absent. Rock markings provide us with an extreme example, alongside the much documented and much mythologised letters and postal rocks of the European seafaring tradition; if they are read as inscrutable remains of a lost civilisation, then they yield a different intertext than if we attempt to think about them as scripts (inscrutable still, but a rival knowledge and writing system). It is worth sitting with Péringuey, there where he is reading these documents and cataloguing these rock markings, just to see how much he is *not* reading where I am reading (of course, the way Péringuey reads may be how I do not want to read, but it nevertheless affects much of the context in which I do read).

The way in which these stones are exhibited today is very different, and the lack of descriptive and explanatory material raises a new set of issues around information and categorisation. While a number of these stones are on display at the Iziko Maritime Centre as part of an exhibition on the histories of shipping in Cape Town, some of the stones remain on exhibition in their earlier home, which used to be called the Cultural History Museum. The building, which was the Cape slave lodge, now has displays on the history of slavery on the ground floor, and has moved the collections of colonial finery, including silver and musical instruments, upstairs. The presence of the stones here is surely a leftover of that previous collection's rationale, since they have little to say about slavery. The stones are in a side corridor which houses the education department of the museum, and the museum visitor is not given instructions about where to find them (in fact I was not encouraged to find them). On the wall behind the stones is a display about flags, the old South African flag rather prominent at the top of the poster, indicating that flags, like countries and ideologies, evolve over time. The stones contain the writing, but there is also another set of markings on them now (their cataloguing numbers and markings), tracing their complex and celebrated histories in collections until today, when they have come to settle here, abjectly unlabelled and abandoned.

Now the argument moves to another version of this same encounter, and with eyes open for the meanings of translation and mutuality in this encounter I look at this same encounter – but in translation. As many scholars have pointed out, Europeans were initially seen through the indigenous Khoikhoi's eyes as migratory beings who posed little real threat because they always moved on again. The marks and letters left on the landscape by passing ships' captains confirmed this pattern, as the messages typically contained information about safe routes, confirmations that a particular ship had passed safely, or instructions to ships about how to increase their safety by sailing together. The letters would lie waiting for passing ships to read them, and then either to annotate and leave them, or to enclose them in packets of letters to be returned to Europe or to stations in the East.

In the pioneering *Khoikhoi and the Founding of White South Africa*, the historian Richard Elphick allows us to review this version of the encounter. In the approach of Péringuey, an approach which closely approximates that of the VOC, 'natives' are presented in two related ways: as either a support or a hindrance to profit, and as the custodians (but not the readers) of letters and documents. The Khoikhoi are described as agents of communication, but frequently their own language is regarded as of no significance – or as many European sources called it, not even a language.

In the writing on this encounter, historians and artists have, of necessity, responded to the written texts (writing understood in the narrow sense here of European alphabetic writing, on paper or stone) produced at the time, since they are the only documents accessible to us now. So this record has been scrutinised not only for what it seems to yield with ease, but also, that which it cannot communicate. In particular, readers have attempted to find in these documents information about the indigenous inhabitants of South Africa and how they viewed the colonial encounter. There are several instances when a Khoikhoi representative is quoted, or where the words and understanding of an encounter are those of a Khoikhoi individual. Not surprisingly, these are the moments in the texts that we, as contemporary readers, find most interesting, and which have formed the basis of much recent historical and fictional writing.

In the chapter 'Peninsular Khoikhoi on the sea route to the Indies, 1488-1652', Elphick reads the same documents that underlie the Péringuey booklet, and finds that they are 'readable' in a different way. Instead of the Khoikhoi voice being untranslatable (or an imperfect version of a European tongue), Elphick's history allows for a way of interpreting this encounter as one in which translation work was done that places the Khoikhoi very differently and allows us to understand the translational contact from another point of view. Crucial to European merchants' understanding of the dynamics of the language encounter is the fact that the Khoikhoi were seen either as a hindrance to, or an aid to, profit. And so the translation work done by Khoikhoi individuals was ideally seen as work that would enrich one side of the communication. Their labour and their knowledge would be harnessed to the advantage and profit of the European trading companies.

It is this interest in information and profit that skews the initial encounter, and renders the translation work that does happen in these early centuries so invisible to the contemporary recorders. Elphick finds in the documents evidence that trade had, until the early seventeenth century, been on beneficial terms to European ships; Khoikhoi were willing to barter cattle in return for what Elphick calls 'miscellaneous junk readily available on any ship' (1985: 76). It is the inequality of the language encounter that is striking. In the encounter between the Khoikhoi and European languages, linguistic gain accrues on the side of the Europeans. Khoikhoi individuals learn fragments of European languages, but the transfer does not happen in the other direction, as Europeans fail to learn the Khoikhoi languages.

By 1638, communication between local men and passing English and Dutch ships had become so successful that there were attempts to appoint local men as agents of the English and the Dutch. The use of Khoikhoi as postal agents provides a fascinating early chapter in the history of translation and interpreting in South Africa. What makes this prehistory of translation and interpreting so striking is the onesidedness of the work of translation, and the sense that the translation was done for the benefit and profit of the Europeans. If one were to write a history of translation studies and the translational encounter, this would be an early example of the effects of unequal translation contact.

When the Khoikhoi became more demanding (and challenged this one-sided profit), writes Elphick, European sailors were outraged, and in fact blamed the translators:

> They put the blame on the shoulders of Coree, a Khoikhoi who had visited England; they suspected that he had given the Khoikhoi knowledge of brass and had told them of the low esteem in which all these metals were held by Europeans … Coree's adventures had begun in May 1613, when the crew of the *Hector* had seized him and another Khoikhoi and taken them on board their Europe-bound vessel.

He was transported to England, where he exhibited little enthusiasm for the weather or the life he saw there and asked to be allowed to go home.

> Coree's wish was soon granted [writes Elphick], as the English, who were imitating a kidnapping technique long used on the West African

coast, intended that he should return home and manage the barter on their behalf. He was taken aboard the *Hector* the following spring and deposited on the shores of the bay in June 1614. Wasting no time, he departed inland with his 'tinckerlie treasure'(a suit of copper armor made for him by the East India Company) and did not appear again as long as the fleet was in the bay (1985: 79).

The English ascribed the resulting lack of interest in trade to Coree who, however, seems to have retained a surprising degree of affection for the English. Elphick writes:

> In the period after the death of Coree our information on Khoikhoi events in the interior drops to almost nothing. This is due largely to the fact that channels of information were blocked by the decline of peaceful barter between Khoikhoi and Europeans (1985: 83).

Elphick makes clear also that communication between the Dutch and the Khoikhoi is vital to our understanding of the period.

Another figure who travels out of the Khoikhoi world (rather than into it, as the European sailors did) was the Strandloper chief Autshumato, 'who was known to the Europeans as Hadah, Adda, or Haddot – and after 1652 as Harry'. His earliest contacts were with the English, who taught him their language on a trip to Java. Elphick writes that the English did not necessarily want to trade with him directly, but were hopeful of turning him into 'their agent in South Africa, keeping letters from one fleet to the next and reporting on the movements of friendly and hostile shipping in the bay' (1985: 84). For a time, he managed to act as agent to both British and Dutch, negotiating with a French captain to remove himself from the bay, and working as a translator to the Dutch on bartering expeditions inland.

Elphick finds, in these early encounters, evidence of the fact that mutual 'information and disinformation' had been acquired by Europeans and Khoikhoi. The Khoikhoi had some knowledge of shipping, could tell fleets apart, and 'several of their leaders had mastered European tongues – a significant achievement, as no European could utter a sentence of Khoikhoi – and had visited Europe or Asia, bringing back tales about European society, values, and skills' (1985: 86). The inability (unwillingness, some would call it) of the Europeans to learn the Khoikhoi languages is a crucial part of this early history. In their wanting to trade with the Khoikhoi (but without learning their languages) one can see a theory of translation emerging where the gain is all on one side, and little mutual interaction is envisaged. The knowledge systems that the Dutch – and other European commercial powers – were part of, excluded knowledge systems that did not contribute to the profit of their trading companies. This early discourse about trade and profit, and how it leads to understandings of communicative acts, can be linked to questions of translation in unequal multilingual settings. In these scenes of contact, the nature of the attention given to the 'translation' is formative for later South African discourse and to the way in which translation comes to function.

In this version of the multilingual encounter, one might expect that the polyglot Khoikhoi would hold power. Yet in the Europeans' inability and unwillingness to 'trade' languages with the Khoikhoi, this inequality instead skews relations to their disadvantage. The Khoikhoi's extra knowledge in fact led to their being suspected of theft and trickery. This imagined theft appears too in the relationship of the Khoikhoi to land. The need for translation of this kind can in itself be seen as a colonial legacy, and unequal multilingualism part of the scandal of the early encounter.

After the Dutch settled at the Cape in 1652, a few Khoikhoi individuals continued the tradition of acting as agents for the Dutch. Two of the most significant figures in this regard are Doman and Krotoä, both of whom had careers as interpreters to the VOC, and both of whom were accused by their own people of being traitors. In recent times Krotoä has featured in a number of fictional and creative projects, many of which want to interpret the translation work in recuperative and ameliorative ways. Both Pumla Gqola in *What's Slavery to Me?* and Meg Samuelson in *Remembering the Nation, Dismembering Women?* explore the uses to which Krotoä has been put in greater detail. To understand these early figures, sometimes called 'translators', it is crucial to pay attention to the lack of reciprocity in the encounter; the 'translators' are in fact more akin to agents, as the early postal system made clear. Their aim is to serve a particular purpose: to pass on a letter, typically (but not always in practice) without opening or reading it and, in acting as the agent, not acting as a possible reader of the message. Other terms that have been used include 'cultural brokers' or 'mediators', terms which also imply a false sense of the extent of mutuality.

In much of the literary work produced in the last two decades or so, and set at the early Cape, this period is mythologised as a place of translation and of mediation. There has been what might be called a false memory of a time before 'we' were separated into race, a fantasy of original mixing (racial and linguistic) or even mixedness. The appeal of this self-forgiving version of history is clear, as are the ways in which it seems to yield a connection to an African mother. In this version, the translators risk being recuperated, once again, as part of a project that renders their own field of reference irrelevant. Histories of translation in South Africa should start with this insight, and acknowledge the lack of reciprocity in these encounters, rather than take the early translators as representing mediators and cultural brokers.

There is another scene of translation in South Africa that has received scholarly attention and come to figure as a moment of collaboration and mutuality, and which has come to circulate as a foundation myth for our scholarship and research. This translational scene is the relationship between a German philologist, Wilhelm Bleek, his niece, Lucy Lloyd, and a group of /Xam teacher-informants. The archive has, significantly for my argument, come to be known as the 'Bleek/Lloyd archive', missing out the names of the teacher-informants, and only commemorating the names of the transcribers. In many accounts of this encounter, the contact is described as respectful, equal, and recuperative of narratives and languages on the point of extinction. In much of this work, we see what I regard more sceptically as a particularly benevolent interpretation of the work academics do. Another, less celebratory, version is to be found in the work of Andrew Bank and Hedley Twidle. Their readings of the material stress that this is not a story of forgiveness and proximity but, instead, that we should acknowledge the closed circuits of intertextuality and the violence inherent in deletion. Bank, borrowing the term 'effect' from Alessandro Duranti and Charles Goodwin's work on language as an interactive phenomenon, places the recording sessions between the /Xam and the transcribers as 'the focal event'. In his chapter 'Early learning with /A!kunta', he meticulously reconstructs the scene of the recording sessions, with all the various stages and levels of translatedness. Paying close attention to the physical objects of the notebooks themselves, as well as to the 'props' used in the transcription sessions, Bank builds up a picture of the 'focal event', which in my argument is also the moment to which I want to pay most attention. Significant also is the fact that Bank calls the *informants* the teachers, rather than seeing Bleek and Lloyd as the central figures. He builds up for the reader what the scene of learning was like, with Bleek and Lloyd as the students who need to be taught how to listen. By paying so much attention to this moment, and writing about the accents in the room explicitly, Bank (2006: 87) also provides us with an example of the accented classroom.

The obvious starting point in attempting to understand the complexities of the learning process in the Mowbray home is the absence of a common language. Bleek spoke German, English, French, and had a reading knowledge of many other languages. Lloyd spoke English, German and French, and had a reading knowledge of Italian. /A!kunta spoke /Xam and may have picked up just a smattering of English from school lessons, prayers and interactions with white convicts at the Breakwater Prison. He also spoke Afrikaans, or Cape Dutch as it was then known.

Bank's interpretation demystifies the process of transcription, suggesting that we read the notebooks kept by Bleek as 'script' rather than 'transcript'. He places Wilhelm Bleek within a European philological tradition, and shows how his system of symbols was informed by the *Universal Alphabet* of Lepsius, an 'orthography created for the rendering of click sounds [which] served as the starting point for Bleek's own efforts to develop a system of symbols to make sense of the complex sounds that he heard in his interviews' (2006: 21). This provides information on how Bleek aimed to transcribe sound onto the page. As far as Bleek's ear is concerned, Bank points out that Bleek's Dutch was at best limited, and a version of Dutch was the 'interlanguage' used with his informants (2006: 24).

Having set out the linguistic registers circulating in the scene of transcription, Bank goes on to develop what he calls a 'grammar of performance', stressing that 'oral communication can be properly understood only in performative context' (2006: 95). Lists of words and sentences may initially seem unfruitful terrain for the application of 'performance theory', writes Bank, but if we study the early notebooks very closely they read 'as nothing so much as a dramatic script. The voices and alternation of speakers may be pieced together with careful attention to detail, tone or content' (2006: 95). Bank's insight into performance theory is suggestive in a further way. He points out that 'gesture and performance were also necessary in the work of translation' (2006: 168). On a session to session basis, 'it is in the interlanguage and small gestures performed before Lloyd in particular that we are able to glean something of the character of the communicative event' (2006: 168). There is a clear link between this attempt at reconstructing the scene of learning and writing, and the work of accenting our teaching and research practices.

What runs through the work of Bank is an insistence on the particularity of each interaction and each transcription event. Writing about the informants' comments on copies of rock paintings, Bank says: 'They said what they did in particular contexts: a specific interview with a specific researcher ... The record suggests that we need to be cautious about projecting these comments as somehow representative of shared concepts. These were clearly subjective readings and misreadings. The comments reveal the importance of taking into account the individual informants' personal history, their relationship with the researcher and – not least – their skill and experience at interpreting visual images from rocks and sheets of paper' (2006: 138). Bank concludes his study: 'Without romanticising the motivations of the researchers or the life histories of the informants, we can recognise that their ability to sustain a decade of dialogue is without precedent in the history of this country and perhaps that of the world' (2006: 397). For Bank, the value of this work lies in the ability and willingness to 'reach out and grapple with a radically alien language and way of life', and to 'submit to a radically alien suburban life where both sides patiently worked day in and day out on creating a dialogue'. In this material, there is an insistence on the work done by the translators, not the transcribers. The archive is not ascribed to those recording the events but, instead, to those who taught them. It is a significant change of stress, and can be seen as an example of accenting our knowledge.

Hedley Twidle has referred very memorably to the 'scandal' associated with the Bleek and Lloyd archive. My tentative suggestion is that the 'scandal' can be interpreted as the very occurrence of the scene of 'discovery' and the attached claim to European primacy. In the recently published *Cambridge History of South African Literature*, the editors have elected to place Twidle's chapter 'The Bushmen's letters: /Xam narratives of the Bleek and Lloyd collection and their afterlives' as the first, in a text where chapters roughly follow chronology. In support of the placement of this chapter as 'origin', Twidle quotes from Alain Ricard's 'Africa and Writing': 'Africa is everywhere inscribed. From rocks to masks, sculptures, pyramids, and manuscripts one needs but a stubborn and narrow-minded commitment to alphabetic writing to deny that the continent has left graphic marks of its history everywhere' (2003: 153). Twidle argues that 'the complex interplay between the oral and written which one finds in /Xam texts has led to them being explored as both a site of origin for, and a persistent presence in, South African literary history ... They emerge as a fitting prologue to an irrevocably divided national literature' (2012: 23). The temptation is, of course, to see these texts as of neutral origin (much the same as Aboriginal Australian stories have come to represent an Australian identity, in a move that obliterates the violence of the colonial encounter).

As a postscript, I want to make a small comment on circulation and circuits of communication. Searching for images of the postal rocks online, I stumbled across a website called '*Die Posklip*' (the postal rock), which seems linked to various white right-wing political groupings and is an unashamedly racist and white supremacist mouthpiece. Having opened this 'letter', I experienced for a moment the shame of reading something which did not imagine me as reader; was not addressed to me; a letter that I resisted being addressed by; but a purloined letter I opened to find written things that should not be read or written. Even after I had shut down the webpage in my browser, the memory of this opening remained locked up in my computer's search memory, the trace of it forever there. It seemed a powerful image of the ways in which our knowledge is not innocent, and of the scandals (as Hedley Twidle calls them) that underlie much of what we know and teach, even when we have not written or received it directly.

Chapter 6

THE COPY AND THE LOST ORIGINAL

IN the previous chapter, the early history of intertextuality in South African writing was mapped out – or, more precisely, the history of an early *lack* of intertextuality. I argued, through a reading of early colonial Cape documents, that the beginnings of European written traditions in South Africa had an explicit agenda precisely of *not* engaging with the local context. The readers for many of the earliest paper texts produced on South African soil – letters, reports, journals – were not local; in fact, the potential local readers were regarded with suspicion, and as a threat to the physical objects that were the written texts as well as to the financial profits they guarded. The second idea in that chapter concerned early translational encounters at the Cape, and the ways in which translation has come to figure as a self-forgiving narrative for current scholarship in South Africa. Through looking at the early translators and interpreters at the Cape, and at a later, Victorian-era incident of teaching and translation, translation was shown to be not necessarily proof of mutuality. Translation often privileges one side of the encounter and silences or disempowers the other.

This present chapter develops some of the insights on translation and its attendant losses and inbuilt hierarchies. In this chapter, I reflect on the histories of our disciplines, and how they might work to exclude a certain kind of knowledge – and a certain kind of learner of course, but that is not the main focus of my thinking here. Building on this work, I try to trace a discourse of staged origin (the origins of our academic and curatorial work, the origins of our disciplines), and a connected discourse of imagined theft as central themes running through South African writing. This chapter is attuned to tropes of theft and obliteration, and to narratives that construct an alternative 'original' that will absolve the translator/transcriber of the blame of the scandal associated with the loss or destruction of the original.

In a chapter interested in origins – their discovery as well as their obliteration – there is no better place to start than a cave. The entry into the cave is a familiar trope from archaeological literature, and one used to great effect in the accounts of many of the great discoveries of rock paintings and scratchings. The person we watch in the creation of her own primal scene, as an academic, artist and archivist, is Pippa Skotnes, whose career, whose very signature, has become entwined with South African cave and rock engravings and paintings, as well as with the Bleek/Lloyd archive discussed in Chapter 5. A common trope in the work of writers on the San is the description of the researcher's entry into a rock shelter or cave, the placing of the researcher's body in the space of the artwork, in the space where the artists used to be. Skotnes often recalls how, with some friends, she was walking in the Drakensberg, there was a rainstorm, they crept into a cave, and here she first saw examples of the paintings. The rainstorm seems to have led her here, to be the (re)discoverer of this particular archive. In another version, she talks of sleeping in the caves and, by inhabiting those spaces, becoming obsessed with the paintings. The need to return to the landscape is a strand in many accounts of researchers on the San, returning to the landscape which seems haunted because the subjects of the research are absent.

There are of course many good reasons for the researchers' need to revisit and physically inhabit the landscape, not least of which is the fact that cave paintings are situated forms of art, thematically and formally closely associated with their landscape. But there is another strand: the need to go back to the 'origin', and to place the researcher in the moment of discovery as the new 'origin'. The narrative of the visit to the cave comes to stand as an enactment of the first encounter – of finding, 'stumbling upon', the moment of origin. In other words, the description of the discovery and the find *are* the new original. It is a trope common in anthropological literature, with the ethnographer as heroic recorder of the last days, who happens to arrive just in time to 'save' a community by recording the twilight of their days.

A theme develops in Skotnes's own work that can best be understood in terms of this concern with originals (that is, originals as opposed to copies). In her work she returns to the question of originality, and singularity (of the rock art); but my argument shows that this discourse of origin shifts, and comes to attach itself to her own signature. It is the originality of her *own* work that comes to occupy a central place in her writings and dealings with others. Her work is interested in the origin and ownership of the archive; and she and her work on and with the archive come to stand in the place of the originals. It is worth tracing the path of this work, or 'faithful work', as Skotnes herself has called it elsewhere. Skotnes has made a huge contribution to our knowledge of San art forms, and her scholarship and creative work force us to view these works as art, as intertextual with other traditions of art. In some ways her project, in its wish to contextualise and to excavate a South African art tradition is exactly the kind of work this book hopes to find. Yet there is another cautionary note in this chapter (and one which may well be levelled at my own work too): that the 'work' comes to stand in the place where the subject of the work used to be. It is an accusation Okwui Enwezor has levelled at Skotnes's work, describing it as a 'colonial errand'; and it is a concern I wish to keep uppermost in the discussion that follows.

When Skotnes first enters the cave, she looks at the paintings as an artist and art historian, and her insight is that she is looking at 'art', looking at the work of fellow artists. It is the meanings we attribute to the rock paintings that first attracts her attention and has since been a recurring theme in her work. Skotnes comments (critically, and distinguishing herself from these other art historians) more than once in her early writings on the relative lack of interest in rock paintings shown by art historians (she is the one who will reverse this trend). But at the same time she is critical of the uses to which the paintings have been put by archaeologists, especially by JD Lewis-Williams. In her writings, Skotnes pleads for a view that sees the artefacts as art and which respects the uniqueness of each image. It is worth here underlining the interest in uniqueness and originality; it will remain a theme in her work.

Skotnes's first paper on the topic, 'Rock art: Is there life after trance?' was published in *De Arte* magazine more than twenty years ago. The readers were likely to be fellow artists and art historians. In this paper she responded to the influential work of Lewis-Williams, writing,

> ... the art might well have come from the heart of Bushman religious experience, but the slightest approach to that heart can only be made by doing what the trance hypothesis exponents fail to do – seeing it not as the illustration of an anthropologically derived theory about shamanism or as mere ancillary illustrations of what is defended by words – but as art with its own unique, formal means of expression (1991: 23).

Her main argument is that while much of the research attempts to dispel the myth of the San as isolated and unchanging relics of a past we all share, the work on rock art 'is intentionally aimed at the search for uniformity and conformity amongst paintings' (1991: 16). It is an original insight, and one that has undoubtedly changed the way this art has become incorporated into a South African tradition. My own work argues that histories of South African writing might need to be reconsidered in this same way, finding ways of incorporating these markings into a non-alphabetic early history of writing. In a 1991 conference paper (published in 1996) Skotnes develops this theme, again insisting on the need to recognise 'the significance of formal and iconographic diversity in the paintings' (1996: 234). I quote here a paragraph near the beginning in full, to give a sense of the kind of language she uses:

> The culture of the people who painted in the shelters of Southern Africa is dead, and in the sense that we have no single testimony from an artist or from a person intimately acquainted with the art as it was practised, it is doubly dead... But the paintings themselves are not dead. In Eliot's terms, they are part of an eternal present. They do not, like science, accumulate significance, they are not superseded, they do not pass out of date, are not superannuated and we must assume that, like all art, they share with the paintings of all other periods the power to affect the lives of their viewers.

The reference to TS Eliot concerns his 'Tradition and the individual talent' of 1921, in which he describes his vision of the relationship of the individual artist to the 'tradition' by which he or she is influenced. Eliot insists on the persistence of the past, its presence in all we do and write: '... the most individual parts of [an artist's] work may be those in which the dead poets, his ancestors, assert their immortality most vigorously'. It is an unusual text to invoke in defence of early South African artists; Eliot is not generally considered a critic and poet who illuminates this kind of record. But in its understanding of the presence of the past, it provides a theorisation of accented intertextuality.

Skotnes develops her own vision of the role of the artist, and her relationship to her predecessors, alluding to Eliot and his version of the great tradition as a cacophony of voices, ever present. The title of her piece, 'The thin black line', is a reference to the technique used by archaeologists to reproduce the paintings, namely the simple technology of acetate tracing: 'Tracing replaces the originals with linear, stylistically arbitrary, monochrome copies, and has absolved the researcher of the need to address the iconographic diversity and stylistic variety that exists in the paintings by effectively eliminating them' (1996: 236). In opposition to this mere tracing she places the eye of the artist, which notices individuality and uniqueness, and in whose consciousness the layers settle on one another. Crucially, Skotnes does not see the Bushmen as our parents, a common trope familiar, for example, from the work of Laurens van der Post; instead she argues that they are our contemporaries. In this she is intending to reverse a hierarchy, and to rewrite art histories of South Africa – certainly necessary, and useful. And yet there is something in this insistence on contemporaneity that empties the cave, and makes 'our' time, the time of the discovery, rather prominent.

Testing and disproving the hypothesis which was developed and popularised by Lewis-Williams that all Bushman art is an illustration of trance experience leads Skotnes to the Bleek and Lloyd archive with which she has become so intimately associated. Searching for support for her approach to the works as individual artworks, Skotnes finds in the archive itself a visual representation of her own ideas about art and individual talent. This is a modernist (she references Eliot, after all) view of the artist as someone perpetually in conversation with other artists, dead and alive. When Skotnes discusses the Lloyd/Bleek archive, she links this understanding of contemporaneity to a sense of the mutuality she finds at the heart of the documents. It is a theme that recurs in discussions of the Bleek/Lloyd archive, as users of it nearly all feel the need to celebrate the mutuality of the encounter. For example, in the conference proceedings of *Voices From the Past: /Xam Bushmen and the Bleek and Lloyd Collection*, the editors write (1996: xx), in language that insists repeatedly on commonality and mutuality: 'The purpose of the meeting was to celebrate the qualities of what have become known as the Bleek and Lloyd records, and to bring together the scholars actively working on them to identify research needs and to share common interests ... The result of the combined efforts of the San (Bushmen) and the Bleek and Lloyd families have produced a testimony in more than 11 000 pages that provides a glimpse into the lifestyles, language and beliefs of some of the survivors of a population that at one time inhabited the whole of southern Africa.'

Having established that the artists of the rocks are 'our' contemporaries, and that their works are examples of unique and original art, Skotnes becomes interested in how we have encountered these artworks in copied form (that is, impoverished copies of the rich and fine-lined originals). Let us look for a moment at the distinction between mere tracing (inaccurate, disrespectful of the individual talent) and Skotnes's own regard for the singularity and timelessness of the artworks. The discourse of originality and respect for the fine line, which becomes so dominant in her work in more recent years, is introduced early on when she uses a phrase borrowed from Walter Battiss, who talked about 'the fine line', by which he meant the 'fine line' of the rock artists. But for me this fine line comes to resonate as the fine line that separates copy from original, 'faithful' transcription from forgery.

Recently, Pippa Skotnes produced a book which included the early sketches by George Stow, alongside her own text and other writings. She called the text *Unconquerable Spirit*, and in it her theorisation of the 'fine line' between the copy and the original is developed. Not only is she reflecting on Stow's copies of the rock art, but also on the reproduction of Stow's work in the book *Unconquerable Spirit*. So she writes that 'the wonderful qualities of high-resolution scanning and fine reproduction enabled readers to gain a real sense of the archive and the scope and breadth of its contents' (2009: 9). Stow's paintings, we read (copies of works which in many cases are no longer visible) have themselves been damaged by 'mishandling and poor storage conditions'. And so *Unconquerable Spirit* aims to restore to viewers Stow's copies; to provide us with copies of his copies, the originals now not even a dim trace. 'Many of the originals that Stow copied have now disappeared or are so badly degraded as to be unrecognisable, so that his paintings are the only reflection of them that remains.' Yet, cautions Skotnes, 'one should not forget that his are interpretations, and not copies that reproduce the originals in any other than the crudest way' (2009: 12-13). Her interest in the originality of the work thus extends also to Stow, and she is at pains to emphasise that his work is a 'faithful' interpretation if not a 'true' copy. She continues:

'While he aimed for the greatest possible truthfulness in reproducing the individual features of the paintings, the demand for fidelity to the original has more recently become so acute that by today's standards his attempts fall far short of anything that would qualify as "accurate"'. The 'demand for fidelity' is a project in which Skotnes herself is involved, arguing for the 'fine line' and the need to respect it. Yet, as I show later, the test for fidelity, for qualifying as a faithful worker has a darker side. Stow's copies have been copied as faithfully as possible. But Skotnes cautions: 'Even with the possibilities of high-resolution digital photography it is never possible to do more than reflect an attitude to rock art, and any form of reproduction will favour one aspect of it over another' (2009: 75). No technology, she is suggesting, can reproduce faithfully *enough* the original work of art. Skotnes's language here gestures to fidelity, but there is a close cousin to this discourse, and that is forgery – a copy that has crossed the 'fine line' of faithfulness, that is too faithful because this faithfulness is in fact a trick.

Several scholars have paid attention to Stow's forged copy of a rock painting of a Bushman hunter dressed up as an ostrich. Stow forged the painting, Andrew Bank argues, 'to promote his view that rock art was simply a record of everyday Bushman life. He wanted his copies to be viewed alongside his bulky ethnographic study of the Bushmen which sought to document their daily lives and customs' (2006: 309). In other words, the fake was an attempt at supporting a truth – a faithful lie, if you like. Bank points out that while many have criticised Stow for forgery, Bleek has escaped similar scrutiny. What Bank goes on to show is that Bleek was interested in the copies as an adjunct to his and Lloyd's work: 'A collection of faithful copies of Bushmen paintings is, therefore, only second in importance to a collection of their folklore in their own language. Both such collections will serve to illustrate each other, and contribute jointly towards showing us in its true light the curious mental development of a most remarkable race' (2006: 310). In other words, the use to which a copy is put also plays a role in deciding where to draw the fine line, and in the decision whether the text is an imposter and new original, or a copy that aims to restore the authority of the original.

Central to the work Skotnes has done is, on the one hand, a respect for the 'original' work of art, and on the other, a model of collaboration between various 'faithful workers', the contemporaries of the dead artists. To whom or what these workers are faithful is of course very significant. My reading is that their faithfulness is to the project, and more specifically to Skotnes's project. In these two strands of her work, there are at times traces of a contradiction. Both discourses rely on faithfulness and accuracy. In its insistence on collaboration, though, I detect a suppression of the chain of circulation to which the previous chapter alerted us. In recent events surrounding the project and its claims to the archive, as Hedley Twidle (2012: 3) has commented so memorably, there is a recurrence of something scandalous. In the light of my argument, this whiff of scandal can be interpreted as the suppression of the inequalities inherent in the very act of transcription, and the desire to place a new (but faithfully copied) original in the place of the 'original original'. Johannes Fabian writes, in an argument that shows how anthropology makes its objects in ways that are not innocent of colonial impulses, that 'it is not difficult to transpose from physics to politics one of the most ancient rules which states that it is impossible for two bodies to occupy the same space at the same time' (Fabian 1983: 29). Using this insight, I want to point out here that the body of the transcriber comes to stand in the place of the body of the original artist; an artist whose demise (or the demise of his people) is not an innocent one. To call such an artist our contemporary is to bring his (or possibly, but probably not, her) work on a horizontal plain with other art. Yet we risk, also, in this idea of liveness, underplaying the reasons why these artists are, in other ways, dead.

In her work with the Bleek/Lloyd archive, Skotnes at once wants to put the reader 'in the situation', and (not deliberately, but this is the result) to prevent the viewer from needing to use and to enter the actual (the 'original') archive. Working with the archive, it seems, creates a scene of paranoia and of hoarding – those who work with this material frequently want to shut the door to others, placing their own 'copies' as the final work in the chain of copying. Skotnes's curatorial project wants to place the reader at the scene, but in the scene that is recreated something has been shifted. She has been there, and has fixed for us the scene, faithfully curated and recreated. But into this scene we may not step any longer, it is now hers to protect and legislate.

In 1993, Pippa Skotnes became involved in a dispute with the South African Library over legal deposit requirements. The library had requested a copy of Skotnes's work *Sound from the Thinking String*, which was bound as a 'book'. Skotnes argued against having to deposit a copy, claiming that the work was not a book but instead an 'artist's book', in which the work is not reproduced but which instead contains 'original works of art', and that this book was 'unique'. The library appealed against the judgement, arguing that even if only one copy of a book exists, the artefact still is a 'book', and that a reproduction (a faithful copy) of the book would not be sufficient. At issue was the definition of what a book is, and also to what extent the 'origin' of a work determines how it could circulate. Skotnes claimed that her book was in fact not a book (but that it could be copied, and that this copy could become a book), and so the court dispute can be read as a dispute about faithfulness and reproduction.

The arguments in this case revolved around signature (is the signature a reproduction or 'the real') and the ability of the book to be reproduced (or turned into a 'copy', whether in fact it was the kind of book of which copies were circulated, or whether it was the kind of object of which each example was an 'original'). The library was not satisfied with 'a copy' (that is a photocopy), and Skotnes argued that the 'book' was an original that *could* be copied; this copy would be less valuable, but would be allowed to circulate freely. So that of the original of the book, there existed no copies; but a self-conscious copy could be made, the status of which would be a copy of a copy. In Skotnes's next project, *Lamb of God,* in a knowing retrospective defence of her claim that her book was not a 'book' she turned a horse skeleton into an artwork that she called a 'book'.

More recently she has published a work called *Claim to the Country,* which includes a DVD that anyone can insert into their computer and there see faithful copies of all of the notebooks from the Bleek/Lloyd archive. As I write this chapter, there is a photocopy of a page from this book tacked to the wall in front of me – it shows a trolley in the basement of the African Studies library at UCT, piled with some of the boxes and files from the archive. The trolley evoked for me another scene of intellectual origin, my own, as I sat as an undergraduate reading my way through the Heinemann African Writers Series. The trolley looks exactly like the trolleys the library used in the early 1980s, and when I made the photocopy, it was this scene of origin I was remembering. It felt as if I 'owned' this image of the trolley, as a ghostly artefact of my own lost origins. In making this copy (this copy which evokes an original trolley, a moment of origin) I was performing a similar gesture, of fetishising and romanticising an imagined scene of origin. The trolley itself would not have evoked this sentiment; it is the beauty of the photograph, the aestheticisation, which invites this fantasy of the beautified and romanticised scene of origin.

The DVD inserted into the back of the book allows readers everywhere to read the archive without having to touch the original, without ever having to enter the space where Skotnes stood to take these wonderfully evocative photographs, and where she was in charge of the creation of the digital archive. The digital copy aims to place the reader in the archive, as do the photographs of the objects; but they also come to replace it, and to replace it with a more beautiful version of the actual archive. Pippa Skotnes's project of digitalising the Bleek and Lloyd archive (or the Lloyd and Bleek archive as she likes to call it) seems to have as its aim to make the documents more freely available, and available in an 'artistic' form. The process of scanning and photographing the material which is included in the DVD (also freely available online) has another effect, though – to take the place of the 'original' (the notebooks in the library). The copyright of the DVD is held, we read, by Pippa Skotnes, and the copyright in the book is stated as belonging to 'Pippa Skotnes and contributors'. The imprint, or 'copyright', page further emphasises the non-copiability of the text with the standard notice: 'All rights reserved. No part of this book may be reproduced or utilised in any form or by any means, electronic or mechanical, including photocopying, without permission in writing from the publisher', making the text the reader holds in her hand one that is precisely the physical documentation of the *removal* of the archive from circulation in this (its 'original') form. Skotnes has been there, now no one else need ever go in again, as we can enter 'her' archive now. The way in which this archive becomes fused with her name and her seeming claim of ownership of it is starkly marked in these all too binding statements. It is the drive to turning the physical archive into a work of art that is what is at once so appealing but also so troubling, in its seeming deletion of the violence and inequalities inherent in the very creation of the archive.

Skotnes explains that what she intended in the first instance was to 'publish and index the major part of the archive', and this is done through the medium of 'technology not dreamed of by Lucy or Wilhelm'. The emphasis on Lloyd and Bleek is rather shocking. While they were no doubt the recorders, and would probably have been interested in technologies of recording, one might think to evoke also the names of those whose voices we see transcribed. Very different in this regard, for example, is the reference to '/Xam (Bushmen and Bushwomen) intellectuals' on Ntongela Masilela's New African Movement website (see Masilela 2004 and n.d.). Skotnes writes that she has in the second instance tried to 'present the reader with something of the experience of being in the archive, of the physical presence of the documents, the shape of the pages, the colour and texture of their surfaces, the signs of use and fragility'. But what we are given is very much Skotnes's interpretation – and a very beautiful document it is although the emphasis on aesthetising the archive is not neutral, and supports my reading of the work as the creation of an origin story, a beautiful beginning where there is neither violence nor injustice anywhere. The book itself, Skotnes writes, is 'an attempt to share this [pleasure] with those who will never know the archive at first hand' (2007: 42). The third aim of the book is to follow a curatorial pursuit, to turn the archive into a work of art (the signature of the work belonging to Skotnes) because, she claims, the visual presence is as important as the text (2007: 43): '*Claim to the Country* with its digital publication also available on the world wide web finally publishes the full collection of manuscripts, making all the stories ... available to anybody wherever there is a computer or an Internet connection' (2007: 44). In other words the 'archive' is created for us in a 'faithful' copy (that is, Skotnes's interpretation); we are given photographs and a collage of documents to recreate for us Skotnes's presence in the 'original' archive. The archive is ultimately turned into a work of art, the copyright of which is held by Pippa Skotnes. It is this drive to beauty that seems to me to be a turning away from accented thinking. In its aestheticising drive it empties out the violence and conflict of the histories.

Despite an acknowledgement of, and dedication to, the 'faithful workers' and 'contributors' to the book, there is a photograph of 'The author at the grave of Lucy Catherine Lloyd', claiming single status for Skotnes, represented in the picture. Picturing herself at the grave is suggestive in a number of ways. The stone gravestone here comes to stand in for Lucy Lloyd ('Here lies ...'), but also emphasises the risk of obliteration – of Lloyd's work and of the archive. There is also an eerie sense in which Skotnes is a resurrected version of Lloyd, a visual parallel she often seems to draw on in her work.

The book ends with one final image, a small key (2007: 390) – and of course a key can be interpreted as something which unlocks, or locks something. In placing it at the end, the key seems to lock the archive to prevent any others entering it, and what we are invited to enter is the aestheticised and curated archive (although one can of course still enter the actual archive – it is not literally locked, it has only been curated).

In the discussion about originals and ownership, the theme of theft comes up again. Theft in academic discourse (plagiarism) can be understood as a failure to translate (keeping something too close to the original, not acknowledging one's debt to the ideas and words of someone else). In some of the 'scandals' around the Skotnes projects, the early discourses of theft and untranslatedness outlined in the previous chapter come up again. There exist, in South Africa, rival traditions of origin and primacy: one of these is the origin myth inaugurated by European scratchings on rocks, marks which enact and perform the extraction of meaning and wealth rather than an engagement with a local context. It is clear how this tradition fails to constitute a South African accented practice.

The rival tradition, that which aims to interpret the other traditions of carvings and scratching on rock, has at its heart still a scandal. In talk about the ways in which we can interpret these languages on rocks, these rock alphabets, we are confronted with the scene of their uncovering and their transportation, as well as the extinction of the descendants of the creators of these traditions. I am not arguing, of course, that these images should not be disseminated, studied and copied, but for an acknowledgement that at the scene of copying and transmission we are witness to the ghost of an earlier theft. The original risks being obliterated, and the moment of uncovering runs the risk of being put in its place as beautified origin. It is a new version of origins that wants to insist on mutuality and translation, but at its heart this version is still compromised by and haunted by its complicity with colonial legacies.

In his work on the Bleek and Lloyd archive (to call it that for the moment, although this very name is what my chapter wishes to reflect on) Hedley Twidle turns at the end, following Walter Benjamin, towards the idea of translation as something which 'not only extends the afterlife of an original but also reveals its instabilities and its suppressed longings' (quoted in Twidle 2010: 189). These words become even more suggestive if one begins to think of the original in these cases as disputed, that the very marking of something as the original is involved in processes of transcription and translation. The original is the source for the copy, but in many cases the copy has disappeared or been displaced.

Originals fade, are destroyed, get lost, are restricted in circulation; and copies can be inaccurate and forged, faithful (or in some cases 'too' faithful to count as a copy). This means that South African scholarship is haunted by the spectre of forgery and theft, of copies that are placed where originals used to be. Twidle writes:

> As a collaborative enterprise of depth, detail and material richness which has been able to support a wide variety of cultural afterlives, the Bleek and Lloyd collection is best explored not as an ethnographic document evoking a banished, mythic past but rather as a body of work continually expanding to include adaptations, translations and literary recasting: diverse strands of writing and rewriting which do not so much explicate from a distance as become part of the archive itself (2012: 3).

And elsewhere (2010: 166) he writes about this same archive:

> When surveying how the /Xam and !Kung records have been brought
> before the public, one is struck by the recurrence of scandal, and to
> such a degree that it seems worth considering how one might go about
> using this unstable cultural process as point of entry when considering
> how such intricate, painstakingly acquired knowledge passes from the
> domain of the specialist to a more general audience.

Many have seen in the Bleek and Lloyd archive the chance to redeem
their scholarship, to find benevolent and redeeming stories about what
academics do. In reading the /Xam interpreters as the teachers, and Bleek
and Lloyd as the beneficiaries of learning, we can begin to turn this around
and to face up to the obliteration of the traditions and literatures South
Africa might have had, the intertextual webs there could have been. To
write a history of South African traditions and artistic developments, we
need to stay attuned to the silences and deletions, and to the violence
inherent in the entry into the cave; and to be vigilant not to make the
entry into the cave a story too beautiful in the telling of it.

Chapter 7

HE PLACES HIS CHAIR AGAINST
MINE AND TRANSLATES

ALL teachers can be said to translate and interpret material to some extent, and this is particularly true of the teacher whose practices are accented. This chapter examines two examples of the 'ideal' teacher's accentedness; and in addition the asymmetries of power and advancement involved in this translation and accenting work. Although this chapter offers the clearest examples of accented teachers in action, it is also the least optimistic chapter. Translation and interpreting are essential aspects of accented learning, but what the discussion below acknowledges is that African languages and English are often not simply different languages through which we gain neutral access to equal versions of the same material. Routes in and out of the classroom are not merely translated versions of one another, and the English language version of knowledge carries its own accents. The 'English' version of a text or a conversation is not a neutral version out of and into which other languages are translated.

The first teacher, or set of teachers, is a group of film facilitators. We see them interpret their educational material to their audience, but they also address the viewer (us) to interpret their work to us. The second teacher is also a guide, and we learn that he has acted as guide in a number of spheres. He is the man referred to as 'Sizwe' in Jonny Steinberg's book *Three Letter Plague*. In this chapter all the teachers are men, and all have one topic: disease and how to care for the body.

The film (*Ask Me, I'm Positive*) follows three men and a mobile cinema making a few stops in Lesotho to screen educational films about HIV and to talk to local viewers about the stories represented on the screen. Two of the young men in the film had been university students, and through various twists of fate are no longer students but teachers instead. They are wonderful teachers, engaging, responsive to context, self-aware, often showing vulnerability – all the things one would want a teacher to be. But of course locked up in these new careers is also a huge sadness, the sadness of lives affected by HIV, and the doors the disease is closing for them even as it opens others.

STEPS for the Future is the name of a series of films (35 films in all), made in a range of styles and in English and several African languages. On the website of the project is a table which maps the language(s) used in each of the films and makes the point about the different language and social contexts in which this film might be viewed – the viewers of the films may have varying levels of education, and a range of possible language backgrounds. The subjects of each of the films in the series are individuals living positively with HIV. The films are educational, but the project is also setting itself against the kind of instructional films to which Africans have long been subject (for an overview of this material in South African contexts see Bhekizizwe Peterson's history of Africans' leisure (Peterson 2000: 127-135)). Some films are available in only one version, some in as many as 17 dubbed versions. *Ask Me, I'm Positive* is available in four languages (although the chart says three – Sotho, Portuguese and Swahili – with English not counted as a 'language version') to reach 'across the subcontinent of Southern Africa, and even further afield', according to the website, in local language versions, dubbed so that people who are not literate are not excluded. The use of the term 'local languages' is in tune with the aims of accented teaching in that it acknowledges other viewpoints and knowledges; but in this table English becomes the language that is considered neutral – not-local, universal. The version I viewed was the 'English' version, where English dialogue was left largely unmediated, although I do comment below on instances where the English dialogue is translated by the provision of English subtitles. In my discussion I draw attention to what one may call the 'versioned' knowledge of the STEPS programme, but also show that the 'English' version is not always equally not-local, unaccented and universal.

The STEPS programme has a targeted approach to teaching: films are made for, and screened, in a particular context. Sometimes this audience is invited to a screening, or is already present (for example, a group of expectant mothers at a clinic). The screening is followed by a question and answer session, sometimes with the people who have appeared in the film as the subjects. The situated viewing and facilitated discussion, as Lucinda Englehart (2003) theorises, provide a perfect example of accented teaching. The makers of the films imagine the context of the viewer, and the value of the films lies not only in the educational content, but also in how the audience response becomes part of the learning. And what better topic for this learning than HIV, one of the most significant subjects young people in southern Africa will ever need to learn about.

When the films are dubbed, the dubbing might remove some of the intimacy of the dialogue, but the films are screened in this way because it is important to show them in formats that do not exclude viewers who cannot read, or cannot read fast enough to follow subtitles. Atom Egoyam and Ian Balfour (2004: 21) remind us that '[e]very film is a foreign film, foreign to some audience somewhere – and not simply in terms of language', and that subtitles 'are only the most visible and charged markers of the way in which films engage, in direct and oblique fashion, pressing matters of difference, otherness, and translation'. Subtitles can be a way of broadening access, but they can also exclude, and they can emphasise difference; they can mediate foreignness, but can also mark it and even create it. One might think, for example, of the viewer who *does* understand the language and is distracted by the disjunction between subtitle and voice, imagining perhaps that there is a subtext to the mistranslation. If questions of translation and subtitling overlay an issue such as disease and its understandings, the implications for misunderstanding are great, and significant. Subtitles, understood in the most straightforward way, are a form of translation. But – building on the arguments about translation in previous chapters – subtitles can in fact bring to the surface the inequalities between languages and contexts. Although this chapter wants to hold up as an ideal the particularly accented teaching of the films, it has another theme: the inequality between the languages of the multilingual encounter.

In these educational films, the settings of the screenings are crucial. The mobile cinema and its live facilitators are a concrete example of the accented work this book theorises: taking material into contexts, finding connections, drawing on communities' identities and shared knowledge. The model of the mediator figure, who accompanies the viewer and interprets the material, is like a situated, context-sensitive, live subtitler – and is in this sense an accented teacher. Scholarship on these films shows, however, that screenings are sometimes not mediated sufficiently, and that the introductions and question sessions are not adequate (Lucia Saks, Lucinda Englehart, and Jane Stadler have all addressed this in their discussions of the films). For example, incorrect and even dangerously wrong statements are made about HIV and left unquestioned or uncorrected – this might be a respectful way of listening to audience members, but it leaves others unsure whether the 'teacher' has condoned the uncorrected statement. An additional concern has been the effect of screening the films on TV, where there is no mediation. Mistakes or misunderstandings in the interpretation of life-saving information are not an incidental effect of the teachers' mediation. In previous chapters the discussion has shown that misunderstanding, staged misunderstanding, conflict and error are part of what will inevitably happen in the accented classroom; the challenge here is to reflect on how they can be interpreted and understood in contexts where the knowledge imparted could make the difference between life and death.

Ask Me, I'm Positive is a meta-documentary – a film about films – which mediates for a particular viewer the contexts where the films are shown. It is a film that places the viewer, visually, inside an accented classroom. It is an example of the activist potential of film, especially of live screenings such as the one we watch others attending in the film. The value of this project is evident, but we can see also the limitations – and the limitations may be where there is most to learn about education and its failures. So, when taking this model and these facilitators as examples of the teacher to be emulated, I do not want to imply that these teaching encounters are without flaws. But there are things we can learn from the failures and the gaps.

In *Ask me, I'm Positive* we follow three teachers (or facilitators, in the language of the STEPS programme) and watch them reflect on their work. The film is, perhaps, not as successful at transmitting information as are some of the other films in the series. Its 'ideal' viewer is someone already informed about HIV and ARV drugs. The important point is that for this viewer, the viewer who thinks of herself as informed and knowledgeable about medical understandings of HIV, there is much to learn from watching the teachers. *Ask me, I'm Positive* is directed by Teboho Edkins, and documents the STEPS for the Future mobile cinema on tour through

Lesotho, screening: *Ho Ea Rona* (We Are Going Forward, 2002, directed by Dumisani Phakathi, and featuring Thabiso Motsusi, Thabo Rannana, Moalosi Thabane and a man known as 'Bimbo') and *Looking Good* (directed by Teboho Edkins, 2005, and featuring Moalosi Thabane). In the credits of these films one sees emerging patterns of affiliation and continued friendship. Thabiso Motsusi and Thabo Rannana appear again in *Ask Me, I'm Positive*, but also appear in the credits for *Ho Ea Rona* (the film about Moalosi Thabane), as responsible for the sound. Elsewhere we read that Rannana used to be a radio DJ (known as Kwasa Kwasa), before he became a teacher/facilitator for STEPS. Working on sound creates continuity with his radio career, and his skill as a DJ influences the style of his teaching. We see him at times 'interviewing' groups of young people, leading them to knowledge through a talk show format. In one memorable scene we see his response to some of the myths surrounding HIV/AIDS: 'Hell man, where do you know these things from?' (in the subtitles, his delivery makes clear that his words are more animated than this bland translation). In the film Thabo Rannana (who is shown as very skilled at drawing out his audience to speak) does not dispel this myth, and this has been one of the criticisms against the STEPS programme.

Thabo and Thabiso appear in the 2002 film *We are Going Forward* and again in 2004 – and one can see changes in their bodies and in their attitudes to their HIV status. The changes in Thabiso in particular become part of the lesson plan, as he can show audiences the difference between himself then and now. The difference is an illustration of the power of knowledge and self-knowledge, the teacher's own healthier body showing the difference this can make. The English version of the film credits a number of translators, including Thabiso Motsusi. We do not hear what has happened to the fourth man, Bimbo, the one described as an 'intellectual'. In the notes to the film he is called a man of few words; perhaps he decided that teaching was not his strength; but there is also the possibility that his illness has intensified.

All the STEPS films start with an eye looking back at us (perhaps thematising the mutual gaze, the need for regard of the other and her position, echoing some of the discussion around the mutual gaze and its limits in the chapter on Thembinkosi Goniwe's eyes). Watching *Ask Me, I'm Positive*, we see this icon at the beginning of the film, but then we are again shown the icon (and hear the distinctive theme tune of the series) each time we watch a recording of an actual screening of one of the STEPS films. We see the audience gathered in public spaces, and the theme tune creates a sense of the repetition and reiteration of the work of these teachers, the need for their lesson about HIV/Aids to be performed again and again. Often, we see the films screened in public rooms, schools or church halls. These rooms already carry in them the promise of learning and its power to transform. Screening the STEPS films in these community spaces and having the energetic and inspiring teachers present, draws on the sense of group identity, but can also reinforce the sense of collective learning and responsibility.

In a scene from *Ask Me, I'm Positive,* grainy footage shows four friends fooling around – three men (Thabo, Thabiso and Moalosi) and a young woman, Libuseng Petlane. The joke seems to be that one of the men describes the other two as 'finished', presumably referring to HIV; and in response he is told he will receive a slap. The men jokingly refuse to let Petlane share their ice cream because she is not 'positive'. In the interview sections, people often ask if one can share food or a bed with someone who is HIV positive, and here the joke works differently – she cannot have ice cream because she is not one of the gang, not because one must not share ice cream with someone who is HIV positive. In a less light-hearted moment, the whole team sit at a table, and Thabiso accuses her of not really being able to understand what it is like to be HIV positive, despite the fact that she is a member of the mobile cinema unit, and spends her time listening to and talking to the facilitators. 'You don't get it,' he says to her. It is a moment when the whole project seems to be in question. If even someone who is sympathetic to the project and has made her career in it, does not 'get it', how can the audiences be expected to get it?

The opening scene shows the friends standing in front of a sign that reads 'Sesotho Media: Mobile Video Cinema'. They are laughing and speaking in Sotho, and the film does not provide subtitles for the conversation. Of course, to a viewer watching the whole film in Sotho, this section would not be noticeably different from the rest of the film; the absence of subtitles would not be noticeable as he or she would be watching a film that is not 'versioned' in this particular scene. In the rest of the film, we (that is those of use watching the film in the 'English' version) are given subtitles for all the dialogue that is not in English, and in some cases we read seemingly tautological subtitles to dialogue that *has* been spoken in English too (and I return to this later). This untranslated moment, however, is one where we are shown the actors/educators off duty, and we are left, if we do not speak Sotho, on the outside of their camaraderie. It is a touching moment, and creates a visual sense of the mutual support in the group, as well as of the private humanity of the teachers.

The next shot shows a red earth road, with the shadow of a moving car and of a camera sticking out of the window. We see the shadow of the hand holding the camera, the silhouette moving along the ground as the vehicle travels along the road and the 'The mobile cinema presents' appears on the screen. In this scene the mobile cinema provides a visual equivalent of the self-reflective nature of this wonderfully moving and engaging film, the camera filming its own movement (the mobile cinema) as well as its own shadow (what is left behind after they go). The mobile cinema is a resonant concept in South African history, and a viewer who can 'read the referent' (to use Simon Gikandi's phrase discussed in greater detail in Chapter 9) is reminded of Sol Plaatje's bioscope, and of the possibilities such a cinema might hold for the future. Lucia Saks (2012: 209) writes about Plaatje's 'project of enfranchising black people as citizens through cinematic means'. This project failed in Plaatje's time, but – writes Saks – South Africans can now write histories and create archives that 'strive toward the impossible, to reconcile with the dead and bring their spirits to life again'.

What Saks argues is that mobile cinemas can act as a means of 'enfranchising' citizens; understood in another way, the mobile cinema could be a powerful tool in accenting viewership. Such archives will bring to the surface accented ways of understanding the past, for it is possible to think backwards, and accent the past. An example of such a project is Hlonipha Mokoena's work on Magema Fuze, in which she not only establishes that contemporary intellectual traditions are influenced by the work of writers like the Victorian Fuze, but that there are ways in which a contemporary historian like herself can read these works and bring them into another tradition. In my terminology, Mokoena is offering us an accented reading of the past, and thereby accenting the present.

In *Ask Me, I'm Positive* the classroom is created partly through a soundtrack, which draws in those we see in the film, but also invites us as viewers to enter the community. The soundtrack of the film creates a sense of a shared world – we hear 'Marabenta' by Wanda even before we press 'play', and the CD or cassette player in the van plays this track a number of times. When the van stops and the doors open, the music flows out of the van (where we have been listening to the music with the men), and begins to affect the people outside. We see small children and teenagers begin to dance as the music is played – from a mobile disco, like the mobile cinema. The music's working is not didactic, but creates community and cohesion. It creates a soundscape for us, those watching *Ask Me, I'm Positive*, and also creates an episodic sense of unity for the many arrivals of the van in communities throughout Lesotho. In other scenes we see the three facilitators joining in with performances of Basotho male stick dancing. Thabo seems particularly engaged in these scenes, taking part while the other men look on, often shaking with the laughter of enjoying the show.

Different is their reaction to a group of men, of similar age, who perform a song about the meanings of masculinity in their context, their singing and actions overlaid with Basotho traditions of all-male ceremonies of manhood. The three STEPS facilitators stand together, looking on, and we (if we are watching the English version and are not Sotho speakers) are left outside the meaning of the song. When the men walk away, Thabo copies their singing, but in English, and inserts new lyrics into the song. His 'version' makes the song one about men who come from the city to talk about HIV. This version (an inaccurate translation) speaks to a sense of something not shared, between Thabo and the singing men, of a sense of being outside and bringing an unwelcome message from the world beyond the Maluti mountains. The film does not draw out the implications of this moment, and the viewers are left to interpret for themselves that which has been communicated in the untranslated (and incorrectly translated) song.

The film documents the arrival of the team at their locations, and shows them setting up their screen and projector. We see the equipment for showing the films, and catch glimpses of the cameras and microphones making the film that we are watching now (*Ask Me, I'm Positive*). In a moment early on we see the mobile cinema being watched by a sleepy young boy, perhaps eight years old (his smile reveals large adult front teeth), clutching a Basotho blanket around his shoulders against the cold. He looks straight into the camera, smiles and yawns – placing the viewer (of his viewing) atmospherically close to him. We watch as the crowd for the evening's performance, including this boy and his similarly blanketed age-mates, collects outside (in this particular community there is no school or church hall). In the concluding scene of the film we see Thabiso sitting on the ground outside the van with three herders, watching a film on a TV screen set up in the back of the vehicle. In each of the outdoor performances we hear the sounds of the evening drawing in (crickets, dogs, goats), and the sounds of a community (mothers calling, a baby crying), creating a rich sense of location.

In the opening scene depicting the screening outside, the camera stays focused on the little blanket-wearing boy and a gathering group of age-mates, and we hear the voice of one of the facilitators/teachers speaking in Sotho (and in the English version of the film we read the words in the

An outdoor screening of 'Ask Me, I'm Positive'.

subtitles): 'We live in a difficult time, a time that requires us as a people to be open with each other. If we aren't honest with each other we will all die.' The audience responds by clapping, and a woman gets up from a group of similarly dressed women. We often see children sitting together, women sitting together, peer groups rather than families watching the performances, which creates the sense of a classroom (age or educational attainment grouping the learners); but there is an added significance in that we see that one is likely to learn most successfully when surrounded by peers – when you are with others who 'read the referent' in ways that support your own interpretation of events. The woman who gets up to speak is old enough to be the mother of the three men, and her question is motherly in tone, not judgemental but needing to know whether Thabiso had been 'naughty' to get the disease. Next comes a man, also older than the three men who are our teachers, asking about what he has heard on the radio, about condoms containing worms. Thabiso answers the question without embarrassment, explaining that this is not the case. Two young teenage girls, hugging one another, smile with open faces at the answer, their bodies close and relaxed. The next speaker is of the same age as the three teachers, and his words mimic their message:

Reactions from the audience to issues raised in 'Ask Me, I'm Positive'.

Production photo from 'Ask Me, I'm Positive'.

If I look about this community, out of one hundred, in my opinion, within the hundred, forty, four times ten, in this village, definitely, among the majority of us, this disease is there. Even if you laugh you have got AIDS. Either you have it, or it is going to get you. That includes you too ... That's right, me too. I thank you gentlemen. You have shown love for our community.

As he speaks, the camera shows us his community's response, sometimes giggling, sometimes looking away, but with people standing and sitting in clusters, comfortable with their proximity to others in the group. 'I thank you, my people. Let us watch the next film,' says Thabiso, acknowledging how the speaker's words have drawn him into their community and supported their work. The teacher brings his story, shares his vulnerability and his knowledge, and in turn finds himself supported by the community. This moment in the film is a clear example of a teacher engaged in accented teaching, versioning the material for an audience, and showing vulnerability and an openness to context. The title, *Ask Me, I'm Positive* provides us with a way of understanding this relationship – for the teacher the act of teaching and the act of being asked (drawn into the community by questions) is part of the developing sense of being 'positive' – and being positive clearly means HIV positive, but also has the other, more optimistic meaning of moving forward through being changed. In this interchange, what we also see is that the transformation takes place not only in the individual, but crucially in the individual's relationship to the community. I return to this important aspect of the teacher's work in the discussion of Sizwe, Jonny Steinberg's teacher while he is researching *Three Letter Plague*.

In *Ask Me, I'm Positive* we are shown a community learning about disease and we are shown the ties the bind them together. Knowledge builds the community, we see, and a community can provide the context for the learning. What we learn is watching them learn – and learning alongside them – about the meanings of community, disease and death. Watching the film, we have an opportunity to experience, cinematically at least, being a member of this community, and to imagine the meanings disease and knowledge might have. Viewing the film like this illustrates the necessity of learning to imagine a context different from the 'English' language version, the version in which medical and practical knowledge of HIV and AIDS is regarded as neutral, not culturally specific. Watching these teachers, viewers of the English version learn how their response to HIV and to the care of the body is something which, in other contexts, is not self-evident and might in fact need to be 'subtitled'. For a teacher, this realisation is the beginning of understanding her teaching as an accented practice. But something more happens to the viewer of the 'English' version: she begins to imagine what it could be like to feel affiliation to this community and to be included in this understanding of community and HIV. It does not mean that her knowledge of HIV in the medical sense is regarded as invalid, but it does mean that she begins to comprehend how what she knows is implicated in patterns of privilege, language and education. To be a member of the community, the viewer needs to imagine sitting in the audience, next to the boy bundled in his blanket.

An intimate breakfast conversation between the three facilitators from 'Ask Me, I'm Positive'.

The film also urges the viewer to take up position alongside the three men, the teachers, and the choices they are making, the risks they describe having taken. Sometimes the filming takes place when they are off duty, not being interviewed by audience members. One particular scene shows them having breakfast together the morning after a party which one of them describes as 'too much'. In this conversation they joke and tease one another, but there is also a shared understanding of the ethical issues they face as – in effect – travelling 'film stars'. Sometimes, people in the audience (and young women seem particularly vulnerable to their evident charms) simply do not believe that they are HIV positive, that their young and healthy looking bodies carry the risk of death. The intimacy of this room, with its bright yellow walls and the food still on the table, creates for the viewer a sense that she (or he – the conversation is fairly gendered) is inside, part of the conversation. The fact that they speak in English for the most part exaggerates this feeling of inclusion.

In discussions about HIV in South Africa, questions of language and interpretation have long been present in some form. One aspect of this is diagnostic: how to read a disease, the meaning of disease, the cultural frameworks one uses to understand disease. There is a large and growing literature on HIV and witchcraft, and HIV and conspiracy theories. Another part of this attention to the meanings of HIV has been centred on former president Thabo Mbeki and his response to HIV – in other words how Mbeki chose to understand (and not understand) HIV and how we in turn understand his (non)-understanding. There have been responses to Mbeki that make an argument about the need to resist representations of black masculinity as over-sexualised; there have been others that interpret his stance as part of his African Renaissance. The repercussions of the AIDS denialism have been discussed in detail elsewhere (see, for example, Mark Gevisser 2009; and William Malegapuru Makgoba 1999).

In Jonny Steinberg's *Three Letter Plague*, Steinberg's guide and subject, 'Sizwe', emerges as someone able to move between contexts – in the spirit of this book, an accented teacher. In what he has to learn, Jonny Steinberg is the ideal pupil, reflecting on where he and his teacher are the same, where they are different – doing the work of accented and accenting learning. This oscillation between sameness and difference has emerged as a theme in this book's chapters, and is one of the important characteristics of accented teaching and learning. In the interactions between Steinberg and Sizwe, as described in Steinberg's book, we learn a great deal about the conditions under which learning best takes place. We also see that knowledge is implicated in the inequalities of South African life, that no knowledge production can be innocent of our histories. Sizwe and Steinberg return in their conversations to these themes, and to the asymmetrical relationship they have to knowledge and the mobility that education can provide. Steinberg reflects on this in a narrative that weaves through the narrative of their growing friendship and the teaching situations in which he finds himself. If Sizwe is a teacher who creates an accented learning situation, then Steinberg is the ideal learner, aware of the accents and versions in their exchanges.

There are a number of teachers in *Three Letter Plague*, and for the reading I give the book it is important to emphasise Steinberg as the beneficiary of the knowledge (as he himself acknowledges and makes clear). The teachers in this book include in the first place Sizwe, but there is also a woman called MaMarrandi (who works as a carer, and a creator of the conditions under which people can live with HIV), and Dr Herman Reuter, who teaches his patients about their medicine and how to live positive lives while HIV positive. Before considering Sizwe, whose role as teacher and whose relationship to knowledge is the most complex, let us look at what we can learn from the kind of teacher MaMarrandi is.

Steinberg meets the extraordinary MaMarrandi, a woman who is not HIV positive herself (and perhaps the facilitators in *Ask Me, I'm Positive* would also tell her she just does not 'get it') but is a counsellor and supporter to those who are. She offers them conversation and encouragement, and urges them to talk to others and to ensure that they create and sustain a role in a community. We read a translation of her words to Steinberg (presumably translated by Sizwe, since we know that Steinberg and MaMarrandi do not share enough language to communicate directly):

> When we came from our training to the villages we were sent to the hospital. We were given the patients the hospital could not treat. At that time, if you had AIDS the hospital sent you home to be cared for by us. And so that was my work. We went to our home villages and we went door-to-door to help the patients to die with the love of their families. We touched the sick person. The family watched. We taught the people how to love the ones who were dying (2009: 161).

Steinberg responds to MaMarrandi, to the version of MaMarrandi Sizwe has made possible for him:

> [I]t seemed that she stood in the space between [the patient] and his pills and gave them their meaning. It was almost as if she took the pills first, chewed them thoroughly, spat them out, and then gave them to him. By the time he had swallowed them, which bit was antiretroviral and which bit MaMarrandi had become indistinguishable. She was the affirmation of the idea that there is a daily regimen that keeps one alive, keeps one's children from becoming orphans (2009: 203).

So in this way of understanding the work of MaMarrandi, caring for someone who is sick is akin to translation or interpreting; it is the reciprocity and mutuality of translation that is likened to the kind of care needed by the sick. If one were to use the language of the STEPS programme, MaMarrandi 'versions' the medicine for her patients, just as Sizwe 'versions' MaMarrandi for Steinberg. In the relationship between teachers and students, a metaphor like this is a powerful way of describing the way knowledge needs to be mediated. At the same time, it is clear that the teacher should learn as much as she can about her student; she can only translate the knowledge if she knows what she is translating into, if she has learned about her student's world.

Sizwe's role as teacher is more complex, and between him and Steinberg there are conversations (and silences) about the meanings of education and knowledge. Steinberg is a university-educated man, a Rhodes scholar and a very visible and celebrated author, who comes to Lusikisiki to do research which will be written up in a book – and in the book he reflects on the meanings of knowledge and education and the inequalities of access we have to these things. Sizwe is a small-business owner, whose parents had ambitions for his education, and who in turn has ambitions for his own unborn children and their education. Between the men is the topic of education, and its links to privilege and inequality. The meaning of education and knowledge is what binds them together, but it is also what marks the difference between them.

Steinberg's Xhosa, we gather, is not good enough to hold a conversation: it is for this reason, in the first place, that he needs Sizwe. In the record provided of their first meeting, the role of interviewer/academic and interviewee/research subject is interestingly reversed. The first meeting between Steinberg and Sizwe shows Sizwe as the one asking the questions. He is interviewing Steinberg, who is allowing himself to be screened as the potential learner of what Sizwe can teach. Sizwe is described as 'strikingly beautiful', and is in a playful mood. He asks 'one question after another', why Steinberg is writing the book, what he wants to learn (2009: 13). Steinberg seems to get the job, and Sizwe proves to be the ideal teacher and versioner. The text describes how Steinberg attends a group support meeting at a village clinic, and is accompanied by Sizwe: 'He places his chair against mine and translates the Xhosa proceedings in a quiet murmur. He is a natural: he listens and translates at the same time, his English unbroken and lively, his intonations performing each speaker's character' (2009: 15). This is a model for the ideal listener, the ideal reciprocal conversation partner. It is also a description of the teacher this book wants to imagine, the teacher who can put her or his chair against the chair of the student and begin to translate – to listen and to translate at the same time. Sizwe's ability to move between languages and between characters is what makes him such a good guide, such an excellent teacher to Steinberg. It is also what Steinberg shows (watching Sizwe and watching HIV counsellors and medical practitioners) to be the most productive mode of being when dealing with an issue like HIV.

As the teacher who provides the work of creating a 'version' for Steinberg, Sizwe moves between languages and understandings of the world. Sizwe's English, we learn, is sound, 'but some of it he learned alone, in the small hours by paraffin light'. So his speech is at times colloquial, at times technical. Sizwe is able to switch between the two languages, Xhosa and English, but for him there is an inequality between the languages and what they represent. His translation work, then, is not equal in both directions. Usually, the translator is more 'at home' in one of the languages, and perhaps mistrusts the other language's ability to represent and interpret all he wants to say. There is too often an assumption that translation results in equality between the languages, between the contextual fields. The non-neutrality of English is a topic Steinberg and Sizwe circle in many conversations. For Sizwe, English is associated with a certain kind of education, a certain path towards the betterment of the self. But it is not without cost, as his growing knowledge of English is also associated with a growing alienation from his other 'language', and his entry into the world that English seems to promise him is always partial, and bears the mark of his unequal relationship to the language and to privilege.

His work is to 'version' his world for Steinberg, but this translation work also brings to the surface the inequalities between them and the place they inhabit in their respective worlds and their shared world. Steinberg reflects (2009: 332-3) on the ways in which he and Sizwe resemble one another and can offer one another a sense of kin and community; but he is also aware of the differences between them, differences that typically privilege Steinberg's world and what he represents:

> The more I thought about it, the stronger my suspicion grew that the history of my own and Sizwe's respective anxieties might resemble each other in the way the chins and noses of relatives do. That the faces are related to one another is as clear as the fact that they are also very different. It would be through the route of the common chin or nose, I began to believe, that I would come to understand better the things Sizwe does not share with me. For his anxiety is obviously modulated by cultural and political forces that are of his world, not mine. But that is precisely what I hoped I would come to understand better by drawing out what we had in common.

Although the work is collaborative, only one name appears on the cover of the book – Steinberg's. There is a record of a conversation between them, one in which Steinberg tries to persuade Sizwe to let him use his real name and to name his village. At issue for Steinberg is the desire to acknowledge Sizwe's contribution, and so he offers him the opportunity to name himself, and take credit for the teacher that he is.

The question of the pseudonym, of a language and name used to conceal, is a theme throughout the work. Steinberg, attuned to the ways in which certain forms of knowledge production make more visible the researcher and his or her agenda (as we saw in the previous chapters), and less visible the communities the work ostensibly serves, wants to bring Sizwe's name into the realm of the known. By making known the real name, Steinberg could display his 'ideal' teacher, right there where he is translating and interpreting. Sizwe's answer is that naming him would place him in the position of informer, not teacher. Retaining his pseudonym protects him from this accusation:

'I would be accused of giving away black people's secrets,' he said. 'It is like what you are accused of when you act as a guide. When Graeme and the bird-watchers were there at their cottage, and I was showing them around the forest, my cousin and I organised a cultural tour for them. We took them to see a sangoma, an inyanga, to see traditional dance, to see the floors of the hut being cleaned with cow dung. They watched the ritual when a goat is being slaughtered.'

'After they left, some people in Ithanga were very angry with us.' They said, 'You go around showing the white people our culture, but they show us none of theirs. You are giving away our secrets to put a few cents in your own pockets. But it is our secrets you are making money off, our culture.'

'I am afraid that I would be accused of the same thing.'

When Steinberg asks whether there is validity in that argument, Sizwe's answer is:

'No. I don't think the whites are going to use our secrets. It is we who keep borrowing the culture from the whites. And anyway, these people who get angry, if they had money to travel to other places, they would also want to know about the people they met there. It is just that they are too poor to travel' (2009: 351-2).

To teach, and to be named as having taught, in this version, is likened to giving away secrets. What is very different in the teaching that Sizwe does and that the STEPS facilitators do, is the place where the knowledge will settle, who will benefit from it. Even though Sizwe does not necessarily agree with this assessment of his work as secret-stealing, the conversation raises the question of benefit, of who is to gain from the scholarship. Reading the book published under Steinberg's signature, we are already positioned on the side of those who are not 'too poor to travel'. In its documentation of his and Sizwe's insights into their relationship, Steinberg's book makes this inequality part of what he writes about; Sizwe's teaching is accented, but Steinberg is also the 'ideal' accented pupil to his teacher.

The book acknowledges the inequalities between the ways (or 'versions', to revert to the language of the STEPS programme) of reading – the one informed by western medicine and the English language, the other drawn from the world of the Mpondo ancestors and the connection to the ancestral land. In the STEPS films, the communities of knowledge and of history to which these men are linked can be made to connect (through careful and skilled versioning and translation), but do not connect automatically. It is in this attention to the work that is to be done to make the connections (as well as the inevitable limitations of such an endeavour) that Sizwe and Steinberg's project provides me with an example of the accented scholarship this book holds up as the ideal.

Three Letter Plague is preoccupied with language and translation, and draws much of its metaphoric structure from the language of bodily symptoms. It wants to ask questions about how to read, how to interpret, how to know which language to use when trying to decode the bodies and motivations of individuals. It is intent on the reader reading elsewhere (reading the body and the meanings of disease, perhaps not reading the book itself). Its understanding of translation and multilingual encounters is not always benevolent, and does not offer the researcher a comfortable position as the discoverer or transmitter of knowledge. It is a work that is interested also in the worth of one's work (as an academic and researcher). The book is in part a chronicle of Steinberg's self-questioning, examining his own relationship to the collaborative work he and Sizwe do, and the benefit each of them is to take from it.

Chapter 8

THE MULTILINGUAL SCHOLAR
OF THE FUTURE

JACOB Dlamini's *Native Nostalgia*, published in October 2009, is a text in search of lost archives, and deeply interested in how we can read and interpret the discourses of the dispossessed. Dlamini, a South African historian living and working mostly in the USA and Catalonia, uses words that seem to have been borrowed from Njabulo Ndebele's significant works, like 'ordinariness', but his arguments borrow simultaneously from another tradition: that of the writers of northern hemispheric nostalgia and the practice of everyday life. This double lineage, as I shall show, does not contradict my initial search for a South African accent rooted in southern African ideas and debates. What Dlamini is showing in his surprising book is that a 'native' tradition (a term he uses ironically) is one that can speak in any language it chooses, and can determine the language for this discourse.

Dlamini looks for a signification system that will enable him to interpret statements and emotions that at first seem inexplicable, the most obvious being how it is possible that black South Africans can remember the apartheid days nostalgically. In his final chapter, 'The language of nostalgia', he raises questions about hidden transcripts and resistant uses of language, and I argue that these are instances of the accented thinking my book theorises. As I show, however, Dlamini's argument comes to include the one language I thought would certainly not be in this book. In the final sections of my argument, I scrutinise the asymmetrical relationship Dlamini and I have to this language, Afrikaans. Developing this insight, I consider the implications of this lack of symmetry for the ways in which knowledge is produced and reproduced and end the chapter with some remarks on the languages of our scholarship, and the implications of language autobiography for the kinds of archives and histories we need for the future.

The life of ordinary things that Dlamini's book is centered on (and especially the remembrance of ordinary things – objects and practices) is part of his project of recovering black history in South Africa. He is a historian in a tradition that documents the subjectivities of black lives, the sensibilities of everyday existence. The introduction to the book includes a narrative based on an interview with two women (and the book is full of women, a feature to which I return), a Mrs Nkabinde and a Mrs Ngcobo. His research trip to Thandukukhanya, 300 kilometres south east of Johannesburg, is to investigate extreme examples of what he calls (in quotations marks) 'the politics of the spectacle' (2009: 1). Despite the quotation marks, the quotation is not referenced. Quotation marks typically acknowledge a particular source; here the effect is instead to point to a collectively held understanding (and phenomenon). The significance for my reading will become clear, as collectively held ideas and meanings remain important in the argument I make here.

Dlamini opens his book with a description of the kind of spectacular politics he is on his way to research ('the revelry, the burning down of government property, the erection of petrol-soaked tyre barricades and the inevitable handover of a memorandum of demands to a government official'). For this purpose, he and a colleague interview 'about a hundred residents, from activists, councillors and priests to the police' (2009: 2). Dlamini is trying to understand the 'causes of collective violence in service delivery protests, labour strikes and expressions of xenophobia' (2009: 2), interviewing residents, aiming to build up an account of collective action. What he and his colleague are looking for is a narrative (or narratives – they do not necessarily want only one explanation) that will make sense, and help them to render the actions *readable*.

So the book starts with an explicit quest – to interpret, to understand causality and significance – but what the progression of the introduction shows is that he becomes interested instead in *another* unreadable narrative, the narrative of nostalgia for the past – a past that is of necessity lived under apartheid laws. In looking for a story about collective action, Dlamini instead begins to see patterns that challenge the 'conventional struggle narrative', where resistance and collaboration are clearly distinguishable, and are the terms through which events and objects are interpreted. Of course in this case the interpretation of the protest is complicated by the fact that the activists in Thandukukhanya in 2007 are protesting against an ANC government, and in particular against the seemingly populist Jacob Zuma (who is later elected president). But in addition Dlamini sees, in his notes on the events and in his own recollections that begin to cluster around these interviews, a fracturing of the very notion of a collective narrative. What ties together these new, non-collective narratives for him is that they are inflected with a particular kind of nostalgia, a remembrance of better things in the past. The fact that the past of this township (and the township of Dlamini's own autobiographical remembrance) was located in the apartheid era makes the nostalgia 'unreadable'.

'It would be easy to bend the sentiments expressed by these men and women to our ideological liking,' writes Dlamini. 'To the leftists who refuse to accept that there is a difference between apartheid and the current order, these sentiments might serve as proof of just how *vrot* things are. To our revolutionaries-turned-rulers, these nostalgic feelings might be nothing more than the musings of reactionaries and even apologists for apartheid. Far more difficult, I think, would be to take seriously these sentiments as one possible way through which we can understand the past and contemporary South Africa' (2009: 11-12). What Dlamini wants to do, then, is to take this seemingly unreadable sense of the past and use its very unreadability as a deciphering mechanism, to try and read the narratives of the past and contemporary South Africa. The 'unreadability' of black people's nostalgia for the (apartheid) past is precisely what Dlamini is interested in. So it is not only the fact of longing for the past that is unreadable, but also the ways in which black experience has been rendered unreadable. That the nostalgia is hard to understand makes it potentially a device for translating (making readable) other memories and narratives.

Dlamini suggests there are at least two sets of interpreting frameworks that render black sensibility unreadable:

> What does it mean for a black South African to remember life under apartheid with fondness? What does it mean to say that black life un-der apartheid was not all doom and gloom and that there was a lot of

which black South Africans can, and indeed were, proud? Only lazy thinkers would take these questions to mean support for apartheid. They do not. Apartheid was without virtue (2009: 13).

Nostalgia makes sense only if one understands that not everything people did in the township was a reaction to oppression (2009: 108). To think positively about black life under apartheid, then is to 'brush history against the grain,' writes Dlamini, quoting Walter Benjamin (2009: 109). The reiteration of 'what does it mean' suits my purpose, to read Dlamini as an archaeologist of signification – how he can read, how he can interpret, the sentiments he notices and remembers. For Dlamini, the key that will unlock the signification system is to resist the narratives (apartheid narratives, struggle narratives) that cannot accommodate these statements and sentiments. The history of South Africa has rendered sentiments meaningless, and it is exactly these surprising and seemingly nonsensical statements that Dlamini wants to 'read'. Related to this is a comment he makes about the fact that the 1976 protests showed little appreciation for the protests of the past (2009: 90), the generational disagreements making the earlier political activism 'unreadable'. (It may be worth noting here, although Dlamini does not invoke this, that the verb for learn and read in Zulu, Dlamini's mother tongue, is the same – *ukufunda*. That means, to be able to read something is to learn about it, and to be unable to read the past means one cannot learn from it. Of course words do not work in this way, but if Dlamini had written in Zulu, the meaning would have been implicit.)

He is at pains to point out that saying there were meanings in excess of apartheid definitions, and that there is a past for which one is nostalgic, should not be read in any way as an amelioration of apartheid thinking. But to accept the definitions imposed by apartheid thinking is to lose sight of the agency that ordinary black people's lives retained. So he writes of the 'corruption of black history', by which he means the propagation of the fiction that all blacks suffered in the same way, that all black people are interchangeable (2009: 21). The resonance with Ndebele's 'Rediscovery of the ordinary' is both obvious and generative. 'It is not often that writers and thinkers take seriously the descriptions that Africans gave of their feelings,' he writes (2009: 129), and it is clear that his project is precisely to 'take seriously' and to search for a language through which to experience and recount this sensibility.

It is an argument that shows a regard for ordinary acts of communication to carry significance, and locates the meanings of lives and of ways of communicating in the private realm (or, at least, also in the private realm). Dlamini wants to insist on that which manages to signify beyond and in excess of apartheid and its languages. The various opponents of this black sensibility, according to Dlamini, have different ambitions. Apartheid thinking had as its aim (both stated and implicit in apartheid thinking and legislation) to deplete and destroy black people's humanity and agency. Yet at another end of the spectrum, in struggle discourse, Dlamini finds an impulse driven by a collective sense of identity. The gains of this collectivity are clear, as are the ways in which such an understanding of identity can mobilise and galvanise resistance. But what Dlamini wants to insist on is the diversity 'within' the collectivity, to find the 'language' through which to express the sensory and emotional experiences of black South Africans precisely there where apartheid did not manage to define and constrain consciousness. And his point is that it was, or could be, anywhere – if one knows where and how to look and listen. In other words, it is an attitude and a willingness to learn that will develop this knowledge.

He tells stories about the Katlehong of his childhood, in fragments and shards of memory. He invokes the autobiographical narratives of Orhan Pamuk and Walter Benjamin – both of whom recount the loss of a particular world. By making this link to foreign writers he is not countering my search for (South African) accented thinking, but instead excavating that which he finds useful in his own meaning-making, through finding parallels in other worlds and times. Crucially, Dlamini's project is not 'nativist' in the sense that it concerns itself only with ideas and identities that are home-grown; it is a vindication of ordinary people's ability to find and make meaning despite, and in addition to, the constraints under which they live. His insistence on the life of 'the senses' is a valorisation of black experience, but it does not resort to 'nativism' in the sense of wanting to insist on 'a' or 'the' black experience. For Dlamini, the important work of the historian of black sensibilities is to construct and reconstruct a consciousness precisely there where its existence had been denied and ignored by some. Black people's sensibilities, literally their senses (and sense-making ability) are what Dlamini wants to remember and explore (2009: 22). This is the accented archive his work wants to curate and to theorise.

Dlamini's insistence on interiority and sensibility is an attempt to maintain diversity, complexity and a sense of identity that is individually determined. His book references a few instances of communication forms directly: television, radio and telephone. When Dlamini writes about listening to the radio as a small child, he is recreating the soundscape of his childhood, but he is also writing about how listening to the radio can be a subversive political act: radio audiences can receive messages not intended for them, or interpret messages not as they were intended to be interpreted. A similar point is made by Sekibakiba Peter Lekgoathi in his chapter 'Bantustan identity, censorship and subversion on Northern Sotho Radio under apartheid, 1960s-80s' in the recent edited collection *Radio in Africa*, and the work of Liz Gunner – on which Dlamini draws explicitly for his arguments.

Dlamini's description of listening to the radio as a child is a trope that recurs in many evocations of childhood, often coupled with a growing sense of self, or the development of language. In African contexts, these memories of the radio sometimes also highlight the disjunction between the scene of the transmission's imagined address, and the actual audience context (see for example Binyavanga Wainaina's autobiographical reflections on listening to Superman in a hairdressing salon in Nairobi, from *One Day I Will Write About this Place*, 2011). Dlamini makes a further point about how radio gave black South Africans freedom of movement, and how the audience of these communications made meaning out of them despite restrictions placed on them, despite not being the imagined audience. The apartheid government, writes Dlamini, could not tell black people how to listen: 'Apartheid planners and censors saw the SABC as an instrument to "shape and control the mindset of its listeners". It did not work. Listeners made of the SABC broadcasts they followed what they willed. Though the SABC could dictate the content, it could not determine the content's reception' (2009: 33). So radio provided the obvious sense of an imagined community (sometimes beyond that of one's immediate community), but it also provided a medium where one could listen, as Dlamini calls it, 'against the grain' (2009: 40). His own political consciousness, he writes, developed in response to radio. He remembers a Zulu language newsreader who used to say, 'There we go again,' or 'They say I must say this …', sticking to the official SABC script but by his verbal quotation marks expanding the reach and significance of the communication (2009: 36) – a rich example of James C Scott's 'hidden transcript', a concept which is useful in a reading of Dlamini's book as a whole and to which I return in the concluding remarks of this book.

Contrasted with this resistant listening is an anecdote about a misdialled call. Dlamini's telephone rings, a man asks who is there and when Dlamini says his name ('Jacob') presumably in a way that is 'accented' to the listener, the caller says: '*Nee dis 'n swart man*'. Dlamini leaves this sentence untranslated, the 'hidden transcript' of its remaining in Afrikaans being clear to any reader. Linked to this is Dlamini's comment on his reluctance to speak Afrikaans to white South Africans (2009: 142). Being invited to speak in a language, a language that the speaker indicates is chosen with irony and with a particular intent, is different from being addressed in Afrikaans by a speaker who asserts thereby a certain hierarchical relationship. In other words, listening to Afrikaans on the radio, or using Afrikaans in private conversations is described as significantly different from being addressed in Afrikaans by someone whose relationship to that language might position Dlamini as an outsider, to the language and to a certain way of understanding the world. There are few neutral positions with regard to language, and this lack of neutrality is part of our knowledge, a knowledge informed by our accented histories.

In Dlamini's final chapter he turns to questions of language and translation, but his choice of language is rather shocking: for Dlamini the language of nostalgia is Afrikaans. I had read Dlamini's book with interest when it had first been published in 2009, and had even made some notes on it in preparation for writing this chapter. When I went back to these notes after reading the book a second time, at the beginning of 2011, I found that I had no memory of reading 'The language of nostalgia', and noticed also that I had not taken any notes on it. My notes made on first reading the book are very similar to those I wrote on the second reading – with one exception, the 'Afrikaans' chapter. It was as if the words were, to me, uninterpretable. My resistance to this argument is revealing.

I had, on first reading, followed Dlamini's argument, which insists on the diversity of black experience and on the need to recover diversity and specificity in township histories. But when his argument wanted to include Afrikaans, the language I have in some ways been in flight from, I simply stopped taking note. Dlamini writes of his reluctance to speak Afrikaans to white South Africans; in my reading, it was as if I could not inhabit this chapter, perhaps could not even read it. It was not that I was denying or disagreeing with Dlamini's argument; it was more a question of being unable myself to inhabit the position he speaks of, of being able to imagine a position from where (for me as well as for him, for me and him together) Afrikaans could be or could become a language in which he/we/I think 'nostalgically'. It was as if, when Dlamini was speaking about (not even *in*) Afrikaans, I was unable to hear it – I could not imagine myself to be the addressee of these words.

There would be positions from which Afrikaans would be taken and used as the language of nostalgia – one thinks of the illuminating reading

Rita Barnard gives of JM Coetzee's relationship to Afrikaans – but from Dlamini this statement takes on a completely different tone and force. He provides anecdotal evidence for why he regards Afrikaans as the language of nostalgia (a language spoken by his uncles and aunts, the language of adults who do not wish to be understood by children, the familial hidden transcripts that knit together generations and gatherings). The adults use Afrikaans partly not to be understood by their children, but there also seems to be a wider social force to the choice of language. If it were possible for black South Africans to give individual meaning to Afrikaans, then that would be powerful proof indeed of the ability to make meaning out of even the direst material (apartheid and its signification system, Afrikaans). It is not only a daring and surprising statement, it is one that is so radical that I found it 'unreadable'. It is a comment that shifts not only the relationship of white South Africans to English (Ndebele's project, and the larger project of accentedness) but also to Afrikaans. If *Afrikaans* can be recuperated as a medium for the hidden transcript, and if it can function as the language of nostalgia for black South Africans, then debates about 'ownership' of the language become an irrelevance and Afrikaans becomes a language of accented thinking and of resistance. The taint of Afrikaans attaches itself to those who claim private ownership of it, not to the language itself – one might say that Dlamini's mother and aunts use Afrikaans in an accented way, claiming it from speakers who regard themselves as 'unaccented'.

Dlamini asks, rhetorically, whether by speaking Afrikaans black South Africans are forcing Afrikaans to speak 'of its origins'. This is of course a possible explanation, but I think it dilutes the force of his argument. There are traditions within Afrikaans (and written in Afrikaans) that assert and even celebrate these black 'origins of Afrikaans'. Historians of Afrikaans were always clear on its 'black' histories, and these are well documented. For Dlamini and his aunts and uncles to speak Afrikaans among themselves (*not overheard by Afrikaans speakers*) seems to me much more radical than simply saying this is a way of speaking back to a not-white history of the language. I had been so surprised and shocked to learn of this use of Afrikaans in Dlamini's argument that I managed to ignore the chapter, and to do the almost unimaginable act of *making hidden* a transcript that was utterly public. If Jacob Dlamini's aunts and uncles can speak Afrikaans to each other, unheard by those who think they own the language, there is perhaps no greater proof of the power of ordinary people to make their own meaning.

'Human beings might not choose the circumstances under which they make history, but they still make history anyway,' writes Dlamini (2009: 145). And speaking in Afrikaans is an instance of this, a way of understanding why (as Dlamini describes it) apartheid suffered the moral defeat that led to its demise (2009: 152). Important here, though, is that speaking Afrikaans among themselves, Dlamini's uncles and aunts are precisely *not* speaking the language of *baasskap*. Were someone who thinks he is the '*baas*' to walk into such a gathering, he (or she) would not be the addressee of this conversation, even though it might seem to be spoken in the language inextricably tied to identity and ownership. This is perhaps the most interesting and most complex part of Dlamini's argument. Any language (or communication system) can be used, reinterpreted, made to signify in ways that cannot be controlled or constrained. This understanding of language users is extremely optimistic about the power of ordinary people's sensibility and the effects of everyday forms of resistance and pleasure.

And this approach to ordinary users of language is perhaps so optimistic precisely because it is not overly interested in whether 'I' have understood or not. The activism of Dlamini's book lies in the ways that ordinary people can recover memory as a process of creating meaning, in particular 'embodied' memory as Dlamini calls it. How I understand his use of 'embodied' is of course with reference to the emphasis he places on the senses, a sensibility that is linked to the way things smell, look and taste, and how people see and hear each other. But the embodiedness also carries within it a trace of other meanings, other signification systems. If Dlamini wants to excavate the sensibilities of (black) township life, then his project is embodied in this way too. It is not a history that excludes on 'nativist' grounds, but one that takes seriously experience and interiorised memory of the body – and in South Africa histories of the body are always complexly racialised.

Dlamini's understanding of nostalgia is one that is closely aligned with his interest in what he calls, quoting Svetlana Boym, 'reflective nostalgia' (2009: 17). In this mode, there is a high tolerance for discord and disagreement. Reflective nostalgia can have longing and critical thinking built into it, and it can find/make meaning where there seemed to be nothing. If reflective nostalgia is tolerant of disagreements and conflict, it provides an excellent approach, too, for the writing of accented histories.

Another strand in Dlamini's work that seems to me to be generative of new avenues of research is the centrality of mothers and motherhood in the way South Africans write about the past. Struggle history often does not account for the activity and activism of mothers. In these mothers (his own in particular, but we see her as a member of a community of like-minded women) Dlamini finds a mode of living that refuses to treat others as a means to an end. In Xhosa and Zulu there are verb endings (-ela, -ana) to indicate this mutual (if not always collaborative) work; one might be able to express a connection that, in English, needs something other than a change of verb. By this I do not mean to imply that English imagines different ways of being (although many have explored this) but, rather, that there are forms and expressions that immediately evoke certain ways of ordering knowledge. If one were to write this same argument in Zulu or Xhosa there would be ways in which the verb itself could express the kinds of relationships the mothers build and imagine. The form of communication Dlamini outlines here is one that does not regard dialogue as merely a means to an end, but which is interested in the transactional codes of ordinary conversations. Dlamini repeatedly refers to his mother as a representative of a 'working-class culture' (2009: 95) that placed a high value on education (2009: 93); and that it was a world governed by rituals that had as their core value treating others as ends rather than means to an end (2009: 99). There is in this perhaps also a model of communication, or of a social world as a form of richly encoded communication, one that can be linked to the ways in which Dlamini has 'translated' the nostalgia that at first seemed unreadable. The work of accented thinking and learning can and does happen in the kitchen and at home, and not only in the classroom.

In this version of communication, and of community, there is not an extraction of labour or meaning from some people; instead the model is one of reciprocity and individuality (though it is not always conflict-free). The chapter on 'The language of nostalgia' opens with 'a person, usually a foreigner' asking Dlamini how many languages he speaks. Five, he answers (Zulu, Xhosa, Sotho, Tswana, Pedi), then mentions the sixth: 'To tell the truth, I should say I speak six local languages, including Afrikaans, but I do not. It is an affectation, a prejudice I believe I share with millions of other black South Africans. We do not care to have it known that we are fluent in the so-called language of the oppressor. The truth is that I speak Afrikaans fairly well' (2009: 135). Interesting here is the consciously denied (then acknowledged) language facility; and interesting also the omission of English. Presumably the location of the questioner ('foreign') lets the reader assume that the language of this conversation is English. Or is English not included in the list of 'local' languages since it is itself foreign, but a foreignness that is unproblematic (compared to Afrikaans, which is 'local' and imbued with meanings one may want to 'affect' not to carry). For Dlamini, English is not worth commenting on, and here his views diverge from Ndebele's, for whom English and its 'local' or 'foreign' status is a conversation worth having.

Dlamini's view is towards the past (he is a historian after all), and to developing the interpretation skills that will enable us to read not only the past but our relationship and regard for this past. When Dlamini finds that resistance versus collaboration is not an interpretive model that can make or generate meanings where he needs it to, his work suggests that new languages, new signification systems are needed – but in each case these will be 'old' ones (and old people, especially old women, are typically the ones who utter or own the discourses that interest him the most) that become readable. In my arguments about accentedness I have tried to think about communication codes that either comply with or resist communication; Dlamini seems to point to another option, that which reflects on and brings to the surface individual meanings that are already there, if only we had the tools to read and understand them.

His evocation of the township where he lived with his mother, and his memory of her beads, her brooches and her linen, provides a way out of 'nativist' excavations of the past, and a way out of narratives that prescribe and shut down what he wants to call 'sensibility'. Dlamini's shocking (to me; it would not have been to his late mother – and this is significant) chapter on Afrikaans is an exciting intervention, one that shows that ordinary people can and do control their own meaning-making, even making meaning through the language of Afrikaans. Dlamini's project is to seize hold of memories of the townships, resisting the interpretation of townships as places of impoverishment and depletion, and instead to recover the richness of signification (that has been there, *is* there already) in the events and sensations of the lives lived there. His book, then, wants to pose a challenge to the master narratives of black homogeneity, and contribute to what he calls the ethnography of township life. He wants to 'make sense' of the township, and to pay attention to the 'practice of everyday life' (2009: 118). His project has, as its ambition, new ways of 'sensing' the township, developing new ways for eyes and brains to interpret (not merely through the 'conditioned' narratives that do not yield enough meaning).

Chapter 9

'A BOOK MUST BE RETURNED TO THE LIBRARY FROM WHICH IT WAS BORROWED'

IN 2002, in the journal *Research in African Literatures*, an unauthorised transcript of a recorded interview between Zoë Wicomb and Hein Willemse, Afrikaans academic and writer, was published (Willemse 2002:144-152). The head note to the transcript reads:

> This conversation with Zoë Wicomb ... took place on the eve of the South African launch of her first novel, *David's Story* (Feminist Press/ Kwela) on 31 March 2001 in the Rosebank Hotel, Johannesburg, South Africa.

Zoë Wicomb did not know this conversation was being recorded, and did not know it would be published; the fact that the interview is in fact transcribed and published places the readers of it (us) in an unusual position – as eavesdroppers, to a conversation about the location of reading.

In this interview, Willemse and Wicomb discuss the book, and also discuss the meanings of 'local'. At moments in the interview, Willemse seems to imply that Wicomb is not 'local' enough, writes from the outside, and is merely an eavesdropper to South African accents and lives. Recording this conversation, the conversation in which he suggests Wicomb is not local enough, and then publishing it without her prior knowledge and permission, he makes Wicomb herself into an eavesdropper, not only (as he argues) to South African lives, but even to her own words.

The transcript of the conversation touches on topics such as the location of the author and the location of the imagined reader. There are moments of discord and discomfort in the conversation, typically to do with the lack of correspondence – or at least an implicit accusation of a lack of correspondence – between the locations of author and reader. The fact that the transcript of the conversation is unauthorised does not concern me here on the level of the ethics of these kinds of recordings.

This chapter takes the idea of the eavesdropper, the reader who is not inside enough, to develop further what a South African accented reading practice could be, and where it could be generated. In this version it is the reader who does *not* read the text in South African accented ways who is the eavesdropper. This argument is tested at the end of the chapter with a perverse reading of the work of JM Coetzee, now, arguably, read as the most metropolitan of South African writers. Not intended as a contribution to Coetzee scholarship, my argument reads Coetzee instead in a deliberately South African accent. This part of the discussion does not imply that eavesdropping readers of Coetzee (those who read him without knowledge of his South African references) are 'bad' readers; but it argues that there are non-metropolitan ways of reading Coetzee that will inscribe him as a South African accented author. There were times in the writing of this book when I thought Coetzee should not be in it, that the attention to his work, and the scholarship on his work (not the work itself, necessarily), was a movement in the opposite direction to what this book wants to achieve. Instead of leaving Coetzee out, though, this chapter concludes with an accented reading of his work. It is an accented reading that could be generated anywhere where a reader is attuned to the local references and traditions. Coetzee is read with an eye open for that version of his work that is (or can be read as) South African accented. Of course this is not the only way to read Coetzee, but this reading turns the Nobel Prize committee and the self-consciously postcolonial readers into eavesdroppers.

But let us return now to the conversation on which we were eavesdropping. It takes place 'on the eve' of what is called 'the South African launch' (implying there are other locations, other launches) of Wicomb's first novel (she had previously published short stories) which is published, we read, by the US-based Feminist Press and South African-based Kwela – in two quite different editions. A comparison of the two editions reveals distinct differences between the market and audience of these two versions of the text, differences related to my notion of eavesdropping. One set of readers (the Kwela readers) are assumed to have knowledge that the US readers are assumed not to have (in my argument, the US readers are the eavesdropping readers, the ones assumed not to know enough about the context of what they hear/read). For these readers, as is the practice with Feminist Press publications, an afterword is supplied, which situates the novel and provides material one might find useful when reading without at the same time sharing the referential field of the novel (its accent). The extent of overlap between a reader and the novel's referential field is of course not clear and simple; there is not simply a reader inside and a reader outside the referential field.

The tone of the interview between Wicomb and Willemse, often difficult to judge from a transcript, seems mostly friendly. In fact at times it reads like a version, a repetition, of a conversation two friends have had before. We gather that Willemse and Wicomb might even have worked together (in different language departments – he in Afrikaans, she in English) at the same university. 'You remember when I was at the University of the Western Cape,' Wicomb asks Willemse rhetorically. They share an interest in Griqua history, they have read similar books (Rushdie, Spivak, Bhabha), they speak in English, the language of postcolonial theory and the postcolonial literary canon – except for one or two uses of Afrikaans words (*oumas, luilekkerland*). Possibly they always speak English to one another and this English-speaking is not just for the purposes of the interview, perhaps there is not, in this particular conversation, an unusual degree of code switching between them, and the few Afrikaans words act merely as a nod to a shared mother tongue – a mother tongue to which their relationship now is very different. Willemse writes and teaches in Afrikaans, in an Afrikaans Department; Wicomb lives her life entirely in English and has never published in Afrikaans. Or, perhaps sensing that she needs to defend herself against his version of her as a mere eavesdropper, Wicomb uses these Afrikaans words as a way of marking her position on the inside.

The interview shifts tone slightly when Willemse asks, in a perhaps unwittingly judgemental way:

> Exile, living outside South Africa, how has that shaped on the one
> hand your writing and on the other hand your perspective of looking

in from the outside? In a sense you're looking at these people as if they're in a glass bowl.

'These people' of course are South Africans, or at least South Africans who still live in South Africa. Willemse's question assumes that Wicomb, holding her pen or typing on her computer keyboard while she is 'not at home' must be *looking in from the outside*. This moment in the interview (the unauthorised, recorded interview) seems like a staged exclusion of Wicomb; Willemse is positioning her (and recording himself doing so, without her knowledge) as outsider. By reading the transcript, we are of course made to witness it, and to re-enact the eavesdropping. And Wicomb is quick to pick up on the assumption that she is excluding her audience:

> That's very unkind. (Laugh) – [the transcript reassures us, they are not having a row]. For a start, I actually started this novel when I was living here [in South Africa] early in the nineties.

Having located the 'start', the origins of the novel with that doubly insistent emphasis, Wicomb loses track:

> So it wasn't written entirely outside the country. I think it's impossible for me to answer that question. I can't tell how something has shaped my view of it. I really don't know because on the one hand I don't live in South Africa, but then on the other hand where do I live? I don't live in Scotland either. I don't know, I don't have that kind of connection with that society. This is all I can do.

Then, recovering from this dislocation, Wicomb asks: 'Are you saying that since I'm living outside the country, do I have a right to represent? Is that the question?' And Willemse replies (but we have no way of knowing his tone of voice): 'I don't think that you need to be defensive about it. My initial question was really trying to define your freedom to write brought about by the physical distance from South Africa and that you have experience of living in two different societies and how that impacted on your writing.' To which Wicomb replies – and this is the part I want to emphasise:

> I don't know whether that distance affords me any freedom. I really doubt it, because I am in denial about living abroad. I say to my fam-

ily, my friends, and myself virtually every year, 'Just one more year.' I really do believe that I'm going to come back to South Africa and live here for good. Remember, I did it before and I had to leave?

The conversation concerns the location of the book (its writing, its origins, the place of its launch), and the location of the author in relation to this. The implied accusation from Willemse is that Wicomb is a kind of eavesdropping listener and viewer and that her relationship to South Africa is something less than direct. The way Wicomb talks about herself in this published version of the unauthorised, overheard, transcript of the conversation is akin to a library book – she describes herself as a person whose return is 'overdue', whose absence (from the place where it 'belongs') needs to be renewed, annually. In the title story from Wicomb's latest book, a book of short stories, *The One that Got Away*, a man called 'Drew' (he has been drawing since he was a boy, in particular drawing in books that do not belong to him) uses his honeymoon to complete what he refers to variously as 'the work' and 'the project'. The work consists of returning a book to a library from where it has been overdue for decades, but it is not a simple return – as one would of course expect in a Wicomb story. Drew, we learn, has long been a defacer of books. In school he dreamed of escape, of becoming 'the one that got away', while his history teacher's voice droned on about what he was meant to be underlining, neatly and in pencil, in the textbook. 'Drew used five colours of ballpoint pen and an HB pencil, leaving none of the text unmarked …'

Drew, on honeymoon in Scotland, spends time in his hotel room 'to work on the book', and the reader imagines he is writing a novel or a short story – perhaps the one we are reading. But then we are unsettled: 'The book *had been* [my emphasis] a green hardback without a dust jacket.' We realise that there is *already* a book, a book that 'had been' something else, something which it, presumably, now no longer is. 'Yesterday,' we learn, 'he had scraped away at the embossed title on the cover before painting it red.' Painting *over* the title, covering the cover. He proceeds to stencil a new title onto the covered cover. The original title, no longer readable on the cover, is *The One that Got Away*, confusingly also the name of the book we are holding when reading this story.

Drew, who must be a conceptual artist of some sort – had discovered the volume by accident in 'the special collection of the Cape Town City Library'. He had been researching the history of mining in South Africa, and the cover of this book (which had nothing obvious to do with mining or with South Africa) was visually almost identical to the volumes on mining – which *were* in the right place, *had* been catalogued and shelved properly. When Drew opened this volume, which *looked* as if it belonged on the shelf, he uncovered the book's original shelf number, the place where it ought to have been replaced on the shelf when the borrower returned the book:

> On the flyleaf was pasted the lending sheet of Glasgow City Librar-ies, and below, Dennistoun Public Library – Adult Department. The last date stamped in the final column of the lending sheet was 16 JUN 1976. Pasted onto the bottom of the gridded sheet was the standard information for lenders about the return and renewal of books.

The date, to a South African eye, is momentous, a red letter day: the start of the Soweto protests, and in present day South Africa commemorated as Youth Day. I will return to this South African reader, the one who gets the intertextual reference not to James Joyce, Dublin and Bloom's Day, but to South Africa, the legacy of the 1970s and Soweto day. Drew's 'work' as he calls it, is to return the book, but he returns it 'renewed'. 'A book, the library's lending sheet instructs, *must be returned to the library from which it was borrowed*'. And Drew, a tourist/traveller himself, thinks: 'Like any traveller, then, the book will return, showing the scars of its journey, the markings of travel and adventure; it should return, flaunting its history and its difference.'

Every borrower of a book changes the artefact slightly, even if only by the addition of a new date stamp. In this case, the book carries a mark of where it has been (the cover that claims it is a book that will illuminate the reader on matters related to South African mining), and two title pages: '*The One That Got Away*, and another before it that reads in the same typeface: *Gold Mining on the Rand: 1886-1899* by Gavin Wilton' (the name of Drew's history teacher). Drew places the renewed volume in the fiction shelf (the volume *itself* is now a fiction). He, we read 'has no difficulty slipping it into the fiction section between Wickham and Witworth. In other words, where Wilton would go, were Wilton to write a work of fiction.'

This is also, of course, the spot on the shelf where *Wicomb* ought to be. And were a reader to go to the shelf in this very same library, there would now also be a book called *The One That Got Away*. Drew places the book here, hoping to take his new wife to the library and to somehow engineer a situation where she takes this volume off the shelf and finds, reads and appreciates his 'project'. She is his ideal reader, the only reader who will understand the intertextual references of his creation – or this at least is his hope. Wicomb leaves the reference to 16 June for a certain reader, the reader who knows South African history. Drew leaves the book for a certain reader, as a coded love letter to his new wife. Instead of a honeymoon he gives her this book, his time devoted to encoding for her his and her sense of place. We do not see whether this love letter reaches its addressee, the story ends instead in Cape Town.

In his essay 'Reading the referent: Postcolonialism and the writing of modernity', Simon Gikandi develops one of the most illuminating critiques of the limitations of postcolonial theory. He is concerned with the ways in which postcolonial theory often ignores local knowledge (although he uses different terms, in a discussion that carefully weighs the meanings of modernity, postmodernity and postcolonialism).

> In North American academies, [he writes], to cite the example I am most familiar with, postcolonial theory has currency only to the extent that it provides a conduit for universalising 'our' theories and applying them to 'their' experiences and practices; representations of the postcolony that speak 'our' language have greater legitimacy than the ones that try to understand these 'other' worlds in their own terms; the postcolonial world has value as raw material for analysis and reflection, but any suggestion that it can be the source of theoretical reflection is often met with hostility (2000: 89).

Gikandi's phrase, understanding the world in one's own terms, is closely related to my interest in accentedness, an orientation that I argue can be learned. Gikandi's concern is with the 'absence of the postcolonial text, its readers and its referent from postcolonial theory' (2000: 90). He provides a striking example of the difference location and intertextuality can make to a reader's response to a text, citing a paragraph from Dambudzo Marechera's *The House of Hunger*, where there is a reference to 'Lobengula's letter to the queen' and an allusion to a character in the story (a certain Philip), as like Shakespeare's Macbeth. Gikandi (2000: 92) writes (and I quote this section in full to show how it links up with my theory of the non-accented reader as eavesdropper):

> Readers easily recognise the second example. It makes an intertextual reference to a text that is familiar to readers of English literature almost everywhere: Philip's unruffled condition is elaborated, powerfully and precisely, through the invocation of Shakespeare's text, a text which

is so common that it is not even mentioned by title. In contrast, the first example is more complicated, not so much within the context of Marechera's novella, but in regard to the assumption it makes about the readers of the text. 'Do you remember Lobengula's letter to the queen?' The intertextual referent is paradoxical because, while it might appear enigmatic to audiences unfamiliar with the history of Zimbabwe, it takes it for granted that the implied reader knows the citation and its complicated history. Any product of the school system in most of postcolonial Africa, and especially Zimbabwe, knows about Lobengula's letter to Queen Victoria: it is both a famous episode in the history of colonialism in the region and a prominent feature of any standard historical text. Within the economy of Marechera's text, the narrator and the reader share a common (perhaps conspiratorial) universe of meanings and evaluation.

But this regime of meaning also excludes the reader who has not had access to the primers of colonial history and historiography in Southern Africa. What often happens when texts like these enter the metropolitan scene of reading is that the first example is not recognised as intertextual both because its referent and primary text is unfamiliar to readers while the second referent, the one from Shakespeare, tends to be privileged and to be transformed into the vantage point of interpretation.

Gikandi's line of reasoning is that there have to be 'protocols of reading' that take into consideration both of these sets of intertextual referents and their historical contexts. In imagining the accented reader as one of the readers, I do not intend to suggest that this is the only reader worth listening to. But it is to say that as a reader and possibly a teacher of South African texts, she or he is the imagined reader and listener I wish to keep in mind at the intersection of possible reading positions. To read in accented ways can be done anywhere, however, where there is the will and an openness to what Gikandi calls 'the referent'. Gikandi writes about 'what the text takes for granted that its ideal reader will know' (2000: 101), and that the metropolitan reader of a text often is precisely *not* this ideal reader. But implicit in Gikandi's model, written self-consciously as a teacher, is that you can learn to read in accented ways, and gain knowledge that will allow you to approximate the intertextual assumptions of this 'ideal' reader.

Accepted as part of this approach is also that 'local' readings will not in the first place be ways of reading with the metropolitan canon in mind. These readers are not thinking about how they stand in relation to the western canon, reading or writing back to it. Instead, seeing these readings as primary, as the ideal or 'ordinary' readings, also means that there is a significant inversion of the weight attached to postcolonial readings and local readings – or what I call accented readings.

This issue is one that Wicomb herself (2005) has written about in 'Setting, intertextuality and the resurrection of the postcolonial author', published in the *Journal of Postcolonial Writing*. By publishing the paper in this journal, its intervention is made in postcolonial theoretical debates, which is not what my own argument is interested in doing. But I read the paper, and Wicomb's fiction, to see what it has to say about my South African accents, and what it means to read not postcolonially in the first place, but to read in the first place in a South African accent. The difference is significant: to read in a postcolonial accent implies an interest in global positioning, whereas accented reading can – but need not necessarily – ask these questions.

In a lecture/reading Wicomb gave in March 2008 at the University of Dundee to a group called the 'Dundee Literary Salon', where she was called on to speak 'as a writer', she claimed that she does not think of her readers, cannot imagine this reader: 'No no no I never think of the readers, if I were to think of readers it would be too painful.' She does not clarify what the pain is. Is it perhaps linked to the pain of dislocation, something similar to what the John character in JM Coetzee's *Youth* refers to when he says South Africa is a wound in him (2002: 116)? Or is it meant more lightly, more performatively, that the author does not know where her reader might be, from where she might be reading, and that this uncertainty about who might read the book is embarrassing, painful in that sense?

A section from Wicomb's *David's Story* (2001: 188) (the book with the South African launch, the book that was started in South Africa) is relevant. When David finds himself in Glasgow (which readers everywhere know to be where Zoë Wicomb lives, adding another layer of intertextual reference), we read:

> Everywhere the names of places at home: Kelvingrove, Glencoe, Aberdeen, Lynedoch, Sutherland, Fraserburgh, Dundee. There was no danger of feeling lost in Scotland, except that he felt dizzy with the to-ing and fro-ing between rain-sodden place names and the dry, dusty dorps at home.

The 'names of places at home' is, of course, ambiguous here: it refers to the names of South African places, but also acknowledges that place names are literally 'at home' wherever they are. But what I am interested in here is when the local (which might in fact be the secondary, derived) connotation seems to a particular reader to be the primary one. In an accented reading of this paragraph, a reader will be aware of the South African locations as 'the referent'. A reader unaware of the South African 'referent' will miss the significance of this geography lesson. This is the reader I am interested in, and I want to see what this reader does in the library and in the classroom, which books she reads and what she notices when she is reading. One would imagine that this reader has been noticed and even feted by postcolonial critics; but as is now taken as a given, postcoloniality's celebration of intertextual play privileges the centre, the cosmopolitan, and certainly privileges those whose currency is English. So the accented reader is overlooked in favour of the reader who is cosmopolitan and whose cosmopolitan reading might include reading Zoë Wicomb's novels, alongside those, perhaps, of Jhumpa Lahiri or Leila Aboulela.

This brings me to one of Wicomb's self-declared interests, what she has called 'situatedness'. In interviews and in her own theoretical work, Wicomb returns repeatedly to the place of the author (and I want to extend her speculations to add the reader to this scene) and the importance to writing of the setting. In her paper 'Setting, Intertextuality and the Resurrection of the Postcolonial Author' (2005:145) she writes:

> The relationship between the *mise-en-scène* of fiction and the writer's physical location has been of little interest precisely because of the orthodox critical position of disregarding a writer's biography. Postcolonial theory does address the question of place, of how the postcolonial writer revises the empty space of colonialism and through writing and naming turns it into place; its concern is with the related concept of identity formation and the link with language. But displacement is invariably discussed in terms of ambivalence, in the separation and continual contact between colonizer and colonized, whereas I would like to focus on a more mundane aspect of place: the *mise-en-scène* or setting of fictions that for any writer is rudimentary, and that for the emigrant writer *can* be problematic.

More than supplementing character description, setting is the representation of physical surroundings that is crucially bound up with culture and its dominant ideologies, providing ready-made, recognisable meanings.

In other words, setting functions much like intertextuality.
She continues:

> [I]ntertextuality, a condition of all writing, strikes a death blow to the author and so liberates the reader from author-centred, theological meanings. Thus the domain of reading and interpretation includes knowledge-based inferencing and an understanding of intertexts and their function in the new context. But for the postcolonial writer it is the transformative effect of intertextuality that is of significance. Frequently our settings in disjunction with citations from colonial texts produce postcolonial irony, and if we are doomed to echolalia it is also the case that repetition re-presents, reverses or revises, or simply asks the reader to reflect on indeterminate meanings produced by citations, meanings that destabilize received views ... What the writer does then is to introduce dialogue between texts, whether they be written or spoken, and so brings into being the interconnectedness of the human world in a divided society.

Wicomb's article argues for the resurrection of the postcolonial *author*, imagining a locus for this author (where will she start her book, where will she publish it, where will she launch it, where will she read from it). But Wicomb's texts also return over and over again to scenes of reading, and to demonstrations of reading that are equally interested in the postcolonial *reader*. In such scenes readers are often seen re-ordering the texts they read, so that reading itself become a reflection on what Wicomb might call situation (of the reader, of the text, of the writer). Situatedness, in this sense, withholds from the reader a comfortable, stable reading position; every reading demands a reflection on this particular act of reading and the meanings generated by this particular context.

What Wicomb is concerned with here is, of course, intertextuality – so beloved by teachers of the postcolonial novel (we think of the courses we know about, have even taught, the countless articles we have read that engage with rewritings of the classics of the English canon). This version of intertextuality privileges the cosmopolitan above the local. It places the author from the local (and I explicitly do not say 'postcolonial' setting, which would imply that the locals are all the same) location in dialogue, answering back, intervening in a conversation that had already started before she arrived.

I now want to test out my theory that JM Coetzee's work can profitably be read in an accented way. He is the South African author who has the greatest visibility outside South Africa, and whose readership has inserted him in categories that include world literature, postcolonial literature, and Nobel prize-winning literature. I am in search of the South African accent in the work. The literature on Coetzee is vast, and this small moment in my argument cannot be regarded as a contribution to Coetzee scholarship, but I want to read Coetzee in a particular way and with a particular accent; I want my reading of Coetzee to be a contribution to accented scholarship and not to Coetzee scholarship in the first place. In a review essay on Harry Mulisch, the Dutch novelist, Coetzee (1997) wrote that 'the chapters devoted to the internal squabbles of Dutch politics of the 1970s are largely wasted on the foreign reader'. One could read this as evidence that local references, accented references, are a 'waste', and should be avoided in favour of a certain metropolitan reference field. Or, and this is how I want to interpret it, one can argue that it is instead those readers who are unable to make sense of these local references who are the location of the 'waste'. In other words, my model of accented reading urges us to acquire the kinds of knowledge that will enable us to read in more accented ways; local references are not a 'waste', but they are wasted on those who are only eavesdroppers.

JM Coetzee's critical essays have been, and remain, a dominant reference field in South African literary and cultural studies. In recent critical debates over Coetzee's work, and his novel *Disgrace* in particular, much of the discussion has centred around the extent and degree of Coetzee's South African focus. I do not wish to rehearse these debates here; they fill shelves in libraries already. Instead what I want to do is to read Coetzee in a strongly accented way, and I do this through looking in particular at two voices in his novels, that of Magda in one of his early novels *In the Heart of the Country*, and Lucy in *Disgrace*.

In his 'Jerusalem Acceptance Speech' (addressed to an audience largely not South African and located, as the name indicates, in Jerusalem) of 1987, Coetzee said (1992: 97):

> The masters, in South Africa, form a closed hereditary caste. Everyone born with a white skin is born into the caste. Since there is no way of escaping the skin you are born with (can the leopard change its spots?), you cannot resign from the caste. You can imagine resigning, you can perform a symbolic resignation, but, short of shaking the dust of the country off your feet, there is no way of actually *doing* it.

The argument continues, interested in the positioning of the white writer:

> At the heart of the unfreedom of the hereditary masters of South Africa is a failure of love. To be blunt: their love is not enough today and has not been enough since they arrived on the continent; furthermore, their talk, their excessive talk, about how they love South Africa has consistently been directed toward *the land*, that is, toward what is least likely to respond to love: mountains and deserts, birds and animals and flowers.

And so, Coetzee writes, if one substitutes love for fraternity, one can begin to imagine a different outcome:

> The veiled unfreedom of the white man in South Africa has always made itself felt most keenly when, stepping down for a moment from his lonely throne giving in to a wholly human and understandable yearning for fraternity with the people among whom he lives, he has discovered with a shock that fraternity by itself is not to be had, no matter how compellingly felt the impulse on both sides (1992: 97).

For Coetzee, fraternity cannot have significance without liberty and equality; and so his speech at this time reflects on the inability of South African writing to express fully an 'inner life' (1992: 98). It is striking how much this rhymes with Ndebele's formulation of the rediscovery of the ordinary, although Coetzee (perhaps inevitably, because of the envelope of 'white skin' that surrounds him and his utterance) is less optimistic about what the path may look like.

Interestingly the piece is collected in *Doubling the Point* in a section titled 'The poetics of reciprocity', emphasising the notion of reciprocity rather than that of 'failure' of reciprocity. The section also includes an interview conducted by David Attwell in which Attwell says (or writes, as the interviews are taking place as correspondence – a mode very different from the recorded unauthorised interview between Willemse and Wicomb) that 'in a colonial situation, the linguistic conditions governing available forms of association are perhaps more visible than they might be under different historical conditions (something the novel [*In the Heart of the Country*] dramatises)' (1992: 59). Coetzee brings the interview back to Magda, and it is in this return that Magda begins to sound a bit like Lucy, another of Coetzee's characters that some have found hard to read:

> Magda is passionate in the way that one can be in fiction (I see no further point in calling her mad), and her passion is, I suppose, of the same species of love I talked about in the Jerusalem address – the love for or of South Africa (not just the South Africa the rocks and bushes and mountains and plains but the country and its people), of which there has not been enough on the part of European colonists and their descendants – not enough in intensity, not enough in all-embracingness. Magda at least has that love, or its cousin (1992: 61).

The parallels with Lucy are clear, and in fact Magda may provide a lens for reading Lucy's inscrutability. Instead of reading Lucy's plot as the plot of lack of choice, it is possible to read her plot as an example of this very desire for reciprocity that Coetzee finds lacking in certain traditions of South African writing and living. Magda and Lucy, read as avatars of one another, reinforce this reading of Coetzee as a writer in whose work there is a trend of a strong interest in accentedness as I have theorised it. Or, at the very least, shows that it is possible to read Coetzee in such an accented tradition.

Read in this way, Coetzee's critical work in *White Writing* is given a different context. The book is interested exactly in this moment of failure (of imagination, of mutuality); and again concerns itself with the failure inherent in writing from the point of view of what he calls 'the master caste'. Coetzee's argument about what he calls 'white writing' is that this tradition has had to base itself on a '[b]lindness to the colour black' (1988: 5); and it does not need pointing out that being able to see this blindness already places one to some extent outside it. Continuing his argument about representation and point of view (or points of blindness) Coetzee writes (1988: 7) about the search for a language that will 'fit' Africa, be 'authentically African':

> Of course there exist plenty of authentically African languages, languages indigenous to the subcontinent. But their authenticity is not necessarily the right authenticity. The quest for an authentic language is pursued within a framework in which language, consciousness, and landscape are interrelated. For the European to learn an African language 'from the outside' will therefore not be enough: he must know the language "from the inside" as well, that is, know it 'like a native', sharing the mode of consciousness of the people born to it, and to that extent giving up his European identity.

Coetzee is writing of a historical tradition, and not necessarily looking forward as Ndebele self-consciously wants to do; but still it is striking how pessimistic a vision this is, how sure Coetzee is that dialogue or translation does not offer a way out of this state in which the 'white' writer finds herself or himself. This could be explained by the fact that the collection does not touch on the period after 1948 (let alone after 1994), and so asking of it the same questions as Ndebele asks of the period after 1994 is not fair. But Coetzee's interest in this collection is precisely with that moment of *lack* of translation, *lack* of interaction that my book wishes to find a way out of, and that I argue Coetzee also begins to develop through Magda and Lucy. His definition of his project is that the phrase *white writing* [does not] imply the existence of a body of writing different in nature from black writing. White writing is white only insofar as it is generated by the concerns of people no longer European, not yet African' (1988: 11). There is another way out of this, I have argued, and that is the pursuit of an accent.

In Magda and Lucy, we see this accented learning taking place (or at least an accented reading can generate an interpretation that does this). Magda, in *In the Heart of the Country*, reflects on the same tradition as does Coetzee, commenting:

> There was a time when I imagined that if I talked long enough it would be revealed to me what it means to be an angry spinster in the heart of nowhere. But though I sniff at each anecdote like a dog at its doo, I find none of that heady expansion into the as-if that marks the beginning of a true double life. Aching to form the words that will translate me into the land of myth and hero, here I am still my dowdy self in a dull summer heat that will not transcend itself (1978: 4).

In *Disgrace*, David Lurie is said to think about Petrus:

> He would not mind hearing Petrus's story one day. But preferably not reduced to English. More and more he is convinced that English is an unfit medium for the truth of South Africa. Stretches of English code whole sentences long have thickened, lost their articulations, their articulateness, their articulatedness. Like a dinosaur expiring and settling in the mud, the language has stiffened. Pressed into the mould of English, Petrus's story would come out arthritic, bygone (1999: 117).

Yet Lurie himself is unable to listen in a medium that is less 'unfit', unable to provide the translation mechanism. It is Lucy's unreadability *to him* that is precisely her ability to perform this process of articulation. The reader, similarly, is forced to question the motivation and the 'language' of Lucy's actions. I am not suggesting that this is the only way of reading the novel, but it is a strand of thinking in Coetzee that has not received much attention.

In Coetzee's theoretical and fictional work there is a recurring engagement with themes of location and address – for example in his enduring interest in censorship. In Coetzee criticism generally, the debates around how (and where) to read him have posited a potential opposition between the local (South African) and metropolitan (international) contexts and traditions. It is in discussions about *Disgrace* that this has perhaps been articulated most explicitly. The South African reception of the novel *Disgrace* is particularly complex, as Andrew van der Vlies has shown in his *JM Coetzee's Disgrace: A Reader's Guide.* Many of the reviews and discussions conflate Coetzee's own position with that of Lurie, but what I want to pursue instead is the model Coetzee develops through Lucy. She seems to me to represent another strand in his work, which is insistent on the possibilities of change and what one might call successful translation. The novel, in the end, thematises the lack of understanding from the point of view of Lurie. But in Lucy there is a yearning towards the model I wish to develop, and it can be used to develop a way of reading Coetzee which shows how his work engages directly with what an accented tradition will look like. And so Coetzee may be the great author of world literature, the Nobel prize-winning author; but there is also a place for him as a provincial author interested in those things that go to 'waste' for the eavesdropping metropolitan reader. In this wilfully optimistic reading of *Disgrace*, I have, I realise, not mentioned the fact that Lucy is raped; in fact my reading of the novel seems intent on ignoring this aspect. I do not pursue the implications of that misreading here, but I will return in the next chapter of this book to another scene where I am shown reading *Disgrace* badly, whereas (maybe even *because)* I try to read it at the intersection. In that chapter, which concerns a university seminar on the novel, I am exposed as a teacher who reads only parts of the novel with her students and avoids the 'referent' that implicates the novel in discourses of what one may call here 'unarticulatedness'.

Chapter 10

THE SURPRISINGLY
ACCENTED CLASSROOM

IN South Africa in recent years, a strong trend in creative and scholarly writing has been one in which writers try to imagine how to step away from South Africa's divisive past, and how to create other, unified, pasts. These imaginings have at times included fantasies of descent that are harmful in their self-forgiveness (a common genre in white South African writing in particular), but have also included challenging examples such as Pumla Gqola's *What Is Slavery to Me?*, where she (not the genetic descendant of slaves) thinks through the symbolic and historic gains of asking 'what is slavery to me'. Such examples of thinking backwards, choosing our ancestors and our teachers, can create paths that lead to the accentedness this book theorises. But this kind of thinking also risks, as I showed in the chapter on the obliterated original, placing itself at a scene of origin that re-enacts a scandal of erasure. In thinking about South African traditions, as this book wants to do, the challenge is not only to write the histories of the past, but also to imagine the pasts we *might have* had. Whereas diaspora theory suggests that the subject longs for a lost homeland in the past, the nostalgia of South Africans is instead, I want to suggest, for a land in the future. Or, put differently, it is a longing for a kind of understanding of tradition that will *create* a past that we can in future think of nostalgically.

It is this complicated longing for a different past and a different future that was the cause of the most extreme disagreement I have ever had with a group of students. This conflict arose while teaching *Disgrace* (in a course on South African films and texts that I was guest teaching at SOAS, the School of Oriental and African Studies), a text that has been the source of conflict elsewhere too. The disagreement had to do with expectations, and with what I perceived to be the mismatch between their and my expectations of classroom conduct. It was a disagreement in which, I now see, I was stuck because of my inability to imagine the classroom in London *and* the classroom in South Africa. I was stuck because of my inability to think backwards and forwards at the same time. In wanting to show students a particularly accented version of South Africa, I became a poor reader and poor teacher. I was so intent on what I wanted the future to look like that I risked turning my face away from the past. It is a temptation we face in much of our thinking and in our teaching. But in trying precisely *not* to think with and about what has made us who we are (apartheid, its histories and tastes inscribed in our universities and our knowledge), we will lose the accountability and self-scrutiny that is needed to develop activist readership and teaching.

In the pedagogical encounter I reflect on in this chapter, the theorisation of the accented classroom was part of what I was learning to do while teaching this course. But it also meant that I was disappointed – and I see now that I was disappointed with where I found myself (historically, as well as geographically). The course was one in which we watched and analysed, at a university in London, films made about South Africans, and in which one of the things we intended to do was to build an intertextual field for the students of South African film and writing. In other words, it was a course deeply invested in accented knowledge.

The students, most of whom had never been to South Africa, had seen many more South African films than any of the students I had taught in South Africa. In terms of scholarship and historical knowledge, the South African accent in the class was developing well. We had watched a number of films that had teachers and pupils as characters, and it was when we were to read the novel and view the film adaptation of *Disgrace* that, by chance, there was some tension in the class around how the student-teacher relationship was to be conducted. The tension had to do with submission of work, and with what I (and some others in the class) understood as a contract that ensured all students had to hand in work on time. The submission deadline was a flashpoint in how students regulated their behaviour towards me (the teacher) and, more importantly, to one another.

A strand in the course reading had been audience response, and the different positions one could adopt when viewing a film. We had spoken at the beginning of the course of theoretical approaches to cinema and audience, and I had drawn diagrams on the board of the complex layers of oppositional viewership one can adopt and develop. We had spoken of resistant viewing, and of the pleasure of not taking pleasure, of being a difficult and resistant viewer and reader. As part of the pedagogy of the class, students were invited explicitly to resist dominant ways of consuming cinema and text, and were encouraged to try out watching 'like a black man', as Manthia Diawara (2009) puts it. So identification (resisting identification, complying with identification) and analysis of such forms of identification were in the room as theoretical concepts. But while encouraging students so to resist, I was also expecting them to comply.

This compliance, as I framed it, was a way of regulating the relationship between the students and me, and between them as a group. No one would be allowed to hand in assignments late and all would need to observe the same code. I framed this code in the language of 'democracy', thus giving an intertextual nod to the material we were studying. I also invoked (mistakenly and irrelevantly, I see now) the levels of compliance expected – and delivered – at South African universities, as if this proved that we should do it the same way. The enforcement of the 'code' also ensured that no student would come to be seen as exceptional, as the special one. I see now that this was a way to enforce, also, the appropriate level of distance between me and individual students. I wrote an e-mail to the class each week, and many students wrote back, submitting their work by e-mail – a degree of intimacy and access, it seemed to me, that risked being too close. As is the custom at this institution, most of the students called me by my first name; it was never discussed, but in a conversation off campus I recall telling a colleague in jest that I had loved the way many students in South Africa called me 'Dr Carli', which seemed to me to convey intimacy and distance at the same time, and placed the students in what to me seemed the ideal proximity. While taking pleasure in teaching the material in London, I was disappointed (I see now) because I was not teaching it at a university in South Africa. This resistance to where I found myself meant that my 'accent' became too strong.

My e-mail to the class, written against the background of mounting tension about 'undemocratic' demands to be allowed to hand essays in late (later than others), starts like this:

> The sections that I am personally most interested in are the ones that deal with Petrus (whose Xhosa name we do not learn). Chapters 14 and 15 in particular. Think about the difficulties of representing this sort of writing on screen, and also how a scene like this will be received (or rejected) in different contexts.

What I want the students to think about in the preparation for the next week is, in particular, representations of black masculinity. The course has circled this topic, and I know they will have interesting things to say about Petrus. But I am also invoking a 'different context', a classroom elsewhere. The e-mail continues:

> Another strand in the text and film relates to teachers and students, and the ethics of the teaching/learning situation. We have seen a number of teachers in our films, and David Lurie is another such a one. In class we may want to talk about the kinds of social contracts that surround and constitute the teacher-learner relationship, what Lurie has to say about it, and how the novel evades or addresses these questions around the relationship between student, teacher and syllabus. Something added in the novel and film ·is the relationship between teacher and parent-of-student.
>
> The section from *There Was This Goat* that I read out to you, where Kopano Ratele writes about what it means to be (and to teach) a student whose whole world needs to adjust in order to be at university, made me think through this social contract. It is not a discourse that rises to the surface often, but one I think is worth considering – and my/our experiences in other education systems can illuminate this conversation. Your understanding of the contract may be very different from mine, and that is OK. And it links neatly to some of the ideas in *Disgrace*, and also to questions of our individual and collective relationship to the material we are reading and watching.

In this e-mail, I acknowledge that my expectations of what the relationship between teacher and students should look like may be different from theirs. But what I want to do, I see now, is to make that difference part of what we talk about in class. I had felt increasingly uncomfortable with my own irritable and sullen response to lateness, late submissions, and what felt at times like lack of engagement from some in the class. I had begun to wonder whether I were misremembering what 'my' students (the students who treated me like 'Dr Carli') in South Africa had been like, and what the engagement and level of compliance had really been like. I wonder whether, in my remembering of teaching in South Africa, I am over-playing the extent to which I was a human being to my students, and they to me. In the disagreements about lateness and compliance, I resent being pushed to make rules and to enforce them, and resent having to defend the code we as a class have agreed to. I resent being made to be a particular kind of teacher – the dictatorial enforcer of rules and the one students try to resist. I want to teach them forms of intellectual resistance, but I seem not to want them to use the pedagogical encounter as the place of resistance. This role I am forced to adopt, as the enforcer of power and authority, reduces my ability to teach, and makes what I want to teach part of a process of disciplining their minds instead of opening them.

I am thus acknowledging, even foregrounding, my particular 'South African accented' teaching experience, and the expectations it created in me. No one ever referred again to the contract (and I have not included it here, and regretted it the moment I had sent it). In an e-mail I sent the next week, I made a list of possible extra topics for essays, still trying to find ways of mending the lack of compliance gaps:

1. Choose a scene (eg Petrus watching soccer) from novel and film, do a close reading of the two and show how the film adds something/interprets/represents/distorts the text. Other examples might include the trial (which a few of you were interested in) or the representation of Lucy, or of Petrus. This writing will reflect on and include class discussion, so the expected level is higher than for a pre-class piece of work.

2. Write an overview of the 'teachers' you have encountered in the films we have watched, and trace a tradition. Why is South African film so interested in the learning situation, do you think? (In the struggle days, there was a slogan 'Each one teach one', an injunction to hand on what one knows. It fits well with third cinema principles, in many ways).

3. Write an analysis of the way SOAS imagines the relationship between pupil and teacher, through looking at the documents made available to students. Relate this to *Disgrace*.

What these topics try to do is to find a way of papering over what I perceive as a growing problem in the classroom – students who do not hand in work, and whose records are falling behind. My essay topics are thus a practical intervention, a way of providing an extra opportunity for the defaulting students to comply. But in these topics, I see, I am also thematising my own sense of my accentedness. I am trying to find a way of talking about my own sense of dislocation and disappointment. In this class I am guest teaching for a colleague and to some extent I am impersonating her, trying to approximate the way she would approach the material. I am a guest. Understood a different way, I am versioning the course for myself and for the students, teaching the syllabus in my own accent. In my speech patterns (my accent too), and in my references, students find a South Africanness that at times supports their learning – they declare that they are developing an intertextual approach to the material and they learn how to relate topics historically. At times, I find myself taking up (or being taken up by) the position of the representative South African in the room. It is in these moments that I often lose my ground, and hear myself wanting to qualify their assumptions and expectations of the nature and degree of my South Africanness, and what my own racialised histories mean. I want to read and argue in a South African accented way, not 'be' the South African in the room.

Yet in this classroom, there is a degree of accented thinking that is more explicit and pronounced than in many (or even most) classes I have taught (or been taught) in South Africa. The material I teach, week by week, makes me long for the classrooms in which I taught in South Africa, the students I taught in these classrooms. In fact it is something other than that: I long to teach this *particular* course in South Africa, to teach the accented material in an accented way, but in that place. In wanting to formalise the 'contract' with these students in London, my pedagogy was not only informed by the fact that I became a teacher, learned to be a teacher, in South Africa; but also that I wanted to thematise the relationship between these students not in a South African classroom and the material, and place their learning next to what my remembered (imagined?) South African-located students would have made of it.

When I look at my notes for this class on *Disgrace* (novel and film), I notice that I have selected only scenes from the second half of the book to discuss, and have left out any of the scenes to do with the university. Central to my arguments is Petrus and his relationship to language; missing is anything to do with the university as a site of learning or a site of coercion. I do not screen during class time any of the segments filmed on the university campus, and certainly not any scenes where the teacher is engaged in his sexual pursuit of the student. In the seminar, our talk is about Lucy and Petrus, their land and their language. I talk to the students about Lucy and that the film manages to show her speaking in Xhosa, but I hardly talk to them about David Lurie – he might as well not be in the book or in the film. My notes reveal that I avoid reference to the fact that as their teacher (and in particular in this phase, their teacher who has to force them to do things that some of them resist) I am twinned with Lurie; instead I want to talk only about Lucy and Petrus.

In my discussion of the book and the film I leave out the campus parts – edit them out in fact as not 'relevant' to the seminar. My questions guide students instead to the parts of the novel that I read as more in line with the version of South Africa I want to present in the classroom. But when we have our disagreement about marks and attendance, I invoke the first part of the novel in my e-mails (written at home, read by them outside the classroom, in spaces where we are not together and not at the intersection of our languages and attitudes) to regulate the kind of behaviour we can have inside the classroom. I am embarrassed by the need to assert this teacherly authority, and I play this out in the arena of e-mails sent between classes rather than in class; I want *not* to be with David Lurie (in the tea room, in the library, setting an extra assignment for his favoured student), who has inappropriate relations with his student, and who is a teacher of a kind I do not want to be – or even to *discuss*, it seems.

I had felt myself placed, uncomfortably, alongside David Lurie in the 'campus' section of the book, as a teacher who sought control and authority and who could extend special privileges to some. What I had wanted was to show the students how our discussion could place them and their viewing experience inside debates I wanted us to have about representing South Africa. I wanted to read the book 'like' Lucy and, through her and Petrus, to imagine a literary and filmic tradition that was not only spoken and written in English, and that was accented. Instead I was pushed into a reading that was more interested in the campus and especially those aspects of the campus (its syllabus, its assumptions) that I did not want to think about, wanted to imagine myself away from and in which I wanted not to feel implicated. An added aspect to this was the fact that the campus used as the background for the film also happened to be the campus where I had been educated – to a large extent (and with some important exceptions) *not* in a South African accent. I wanted in the SOAS seminar to impersonate (or to version, in the language of the

STEPS teachers) a South African of the kind I have tried to imagine in this book. Instead, I was reminded of how we are also determined by the other meanings of the university, those that are complicit in and formed by another history. I was subconsciously wanting to distance myself from the past, from a particular version of the university and its institutional legacies, and from a version of South African history; and in doing that I misread and misrepresented the material.

This encounter, which seemed to be about marks and marking procedures but was also about the relationship between teachers, students and knowledge, brought me to think again about my relationship to my own education, to the teachers I did have (in the early days of being taught African literature in an English department in South Africa, by teachers who transformed my world – including JM Coetzee, the author I was misreading so convolutedly in this seminar). But it also made me think of the teachers I did *not* have, could not have had because of the violent separation of bodies and knowledge that was apartheid.

At around the same time I came across a photograph of a young Ntongela Masilela, then professor of English and World literature at Pitzer College in the USA. The photograph is from his website on the New African Movement and shows him, aged 32, 'in Poland' at around the time I finished school and first went to university.

Masilela's website is a portal through which we can enter another version of our history, looking backwards and forwards at the same time. He writes, in an interview that introduces the website:

> The dramatic political changes that happened in our country in 1994 compelled me to attempt to reconstruct South African intellectual and cultural history, a legacy that has been made invisible by politics of domination, i.e., apartheid and segregation.

Later in the interview he says that 'the first fundamental reason for constructing this website of the New African Movement was to share first and foremost with my compatriots and with other people in the world our intellectual legacy'; the second reason was to 'construct a map of the entrance through violence of European modernity (through imperialism and colonialism) and its subsequent transformation into South African modernity' (2004: 12). Masilela's project is thus framed as one of construction (of a website, of a tradition, of a map to an entrance). But his map has been made with a student in mind:

... I want to emphasise that my singular intent with the website is to restore our political and cultural traditions in a form that would be user-friendly to students and scholars all over the world. I hope the website will resonate with the intellectual curiosity of the students whatever their level of maturity. I hope they will find something that is compatible with their intellectual interests ... Although the website was aimed at students, it was constructed in such a manner that it would also serve the intellectual and emotional needs of scholars as well as of the general public.

To this end, Masilela imagines a range of 'portals' (a commonly used word in web design, but here resonant in its reference to entry), and a range of possible entry points. His first imagined reader is a pre-literate primary school pupil looking at the photographs as a way of being introduced to 'the figures of our intellectual tradition'. The website has many doors, or portals; and, following on from the architectural metaphors, it is imagined as something that can never be completed: 'it is for visitors to carry on its further construction in their own particular ways'. The interview ends with the words: 'This website has been patiently constructed in such a way that no South African can claim with good conscience that he or she is not knowledgeable about our intellectual and cultural traditions because they are not easily available in an accessible manner.' The aim of these words is to introduce, to invite the learner to enter. But there is also a challenge in these words: the work has begun, and it is up to us now. The location of this work, we read at the bottom of the interview, is 'Johannesburg, South Africa-Claremont [Los Angeles], California, July 3-4, 2004'. Reading through the archive collected on the New African website, I see gathered together many of the things I could have learned had Masilela been my teacher in the 1980s (and did not learn then). But the location of the knowledge (California, the Internet) shows that a South African accented learning and teaching practice can happen anywhere, wherever there is the will. Recognising that the work of accenting can happen anywhere is an optimistic response, forward-looking and positive. But part of the work of accenting our traditions and our futures will need to be insistent on conflict and difficulty, and on the historical absence of certain teachers and texts from South African classrooms. South African intellectual traditions, writing and art are shaped by absences and gaps, by the spaces where should have been the careers and lives interrupted by apartheid, discrimination and sometimes exile.

Concluding remarks

This book has offered a defence of difficulty, of failure and of misunderstanding. It has argued that the long ending of apartheid can only be brought about by a high degree of tolerance for difference and for disagreement. Accented thinking, as it has been theorised in these pages, brings difference to the surface, and does not strive for a unified and unitary position. Therefore the reasoning in this book has been about moments of conflict and non-agreement as possible sites of learning and transformation. With such an approach, instances of disagreement and misunderstanding become rich with potential instead of providing the instances of breakdown or failure that lead to silence. Disagreement, and the discussion and acknowledgment of disagreement, are held up in this book as a version of ideal classroom practice, where the lessons that are learned do not strive to create unity or agreement.

In the recently published *The Cambridge History of South African Literature*, the editors open the work with a section on racial classification, 'Note on racial nomenclature and languages' (Attridge and Attwell 2012: xvii): 'The history of racial classification in South Africa makes it necessary to use terms referring to different racial groups; this is done without any implication that these categorisations have a scientific basis.' This note is included partly for an international audience – South African texts intended for an international audience often carry such notes, describing to others what South Africans may disagree with, but always assume and know intuitively. In this case, the editors have also included these notes as a way of talking through the ways in which knowledge has been ordered in South Africa. The *Cambridge History* reflects on the way 'we' have been categorised, and also on how knowledge about 'our' traditions has been categorised in an unwitting re-enactment of the imposed classifications. The editors offer a multiauthored perspective, and allow traditions that have developed alongside one another to crash into one another, reading works in the new contexts provided by mapping adjacency. They take the view that the history of each of the country's literatures appears in a different light when viewed in the context of the others, even when there is no explicit influence or shared traditions.

In this way, the *Cambridge History of South African Literature* moves away from the limitations and inevitable disappointments of a search for a unified national tradition in which influences can be traced. It acknowledges instead what is often the intellectual violence of a *lack* of influences and a lack of intertextuality, the implications of ignorance between languages and creative traditions in South Africa. The editors take for granted that South African writing (and South African people) have a 'unifying history', even a 'national mythology'. But this does not imply a history of unity; on the contrary, they write 'South Africans generally understand what they disagree about'. The various literatures in South Africa 'do speak to one another but when they *fail* to do so, this failure is no less significant as we seek to understand the complexity of the picture' (Attridge and Attwell 2012: xvii).

Difficulties and miscommunications, misunderstandings and failures, my book has tried to suggest, are thus to be tolerated and even welcomed. Crucially, these moments are to be seen for what they reveal about the apartheid past's enduring reach. It is in the insistence on our differences, and in facing up to the enduring legacy of apartheid, that its end might be brought about. In *Domination and the Arts of Resistance: Hidden Transcripts*, James C Scott (1990: 5) writes of the discrepancy between what he calls the hidden transcript and the public transcript used by people in situations where they are subjugated. This is an argument that seems at first to offer us more in the way of understanding resistance during the most restrictive days of the apartheid era. He chronicles the everyday acts of verbal resistance that can be found in the language use of subjugated groups. When such individuals speak to one another within hearing of those in power, he argues, they use a private transcript which consists of 'those offstage speeches, gestures, and practices that confirm, contradict, or inflect what appears in the public transcript'. In much of his book, he analyses situations where the need for a hidden transcript exists, but where these everyday acts of resistance remain hidden (the public transcript does not challenge power relations).

The final chapter of Scott's book concerns what he calls 'the first public declaration of the hidden transcript' which becomes visible when there is a disruption, where the powerless break their silence and rupture the seemingly calm surface. The locations of the hidden transcript, Scott writes in this final chapter, include the 'unspoken riposte, stifled anger, and bitten tongues' (2009: 120). My own theorisation of the development of accented discourse can be seen as an investigation of this historical moment, the time of ruptures and of 'first declarations'. Scott argues further that the moment of rupture should be understood in terms of its prehistory, the prehistory of its life as a hidden transcript. In these moments, those who have been the dispossessed and powerless speak not only of the moment of rupture – their words and actions also carry the explicit prehistories of their domination. For this reason, the ruptures can take the form of staged behaviour, as I have argued in a number of the chapters in this book. These performances of misunderstanding, conflict, failure and anger are best understood if we view them as examples of what Scott calls the rupturing event. In the statements and actions that are characterised as expressions of the rupture, there is an insistence on the enduring effects of the previous time (for Scott, the previous times of the places and peoples about whom he writes; for me the colonial past and its persistence), which may at times seem at odds with the current state of power relations. It is this insistence on the presence of the past that makes these accented actions and statements so nonconciliatory and so fraught with accusations of misunderstanding and misperception.

For Scott, the 'public declaration of the hidden transcript, because it supplies a part of a person's character that has earlier been kept safely out of sight, seems also to restore a sense of self-respect and personhood' (2009: 210). And the satisfaction in this process depends on the process being acknowledged, and made public. The hidden histories of resistance and domination are brought to the surface to become part of the new archive. In order to write histories of South Africa that can allow what Scott calls the 'hidden transcripts' to be excavated, it is the loud and angry voices that need to be heard for what they can tell of the past. Even if these conflicts seem not to respond to a present context, they should be understood as acts of resistance and defiance, and this anger is part of how we are to understand the present – the time of rupture – and on which we are to build our accented futures.

In contrast with this understanding of the long ending of apartheid as a time of rupture and of new archives of anger, is the way this time is imagined in a historical document that spoke of this time as a future, the 1955 Kliptown Charter:

The doors of learning and culture shall be opened!

The government shall discover, develop and encourage national talent for the enhancement of cultural life;

All the cultural treasures of mankind shall be open to all, by free exchange of books, ideas and contact with other lands;

The aim of education shall be to teach the youth to love their people and their culture, to honour human brotherhood, liberty and peace;

Education shall be free, compulsory, universal and equal for all children;

Higher education and technical training shall be opened to all by means of state allowances and scholarships awarded on the basis of merit;

Adult illiteracy shall be ended by a mass state educational plan;

Teachers shall have all the rights of other citizens;

The colour bar in cultural life, in sport and in education shall be abolished.

Spoken and formulated in the spirit of revolution, the Freedom Charter envisioned, from its vantage point in 1955, a different future for black South Africans. The language is forward-looking, the verb forms certain of that moment in the future when all 'shall' be as hoped. One may want to insist that the portal, and the doors, have not yet opened, but that they are opening. The authors, critics, artists and readers in the chapters in this book are involved in the work of opening, the activist work of ending apartheid and creating from the ruin new accented archives and new traditions. This book has argued that such work will not always be positive and conciliatory; at times conflict, misunderstanding and disagreement will be dominant, but out of this will, one hopes, come a willingness to reveal vulnerability and a willingness to learn. There is no way of constructing a portal without acknowledging the conflict from our histories, and to do so would be to turn away from how the present is still informed by the past.

References

Alcoff, Linda Martin (2006) *Visible Identities: Race, Gender and the Self.* Oxford: Oxford University Press.

Apter, Emily (2006) *The Translation Zone: A New Comparative Literature.* Princeton: Princeton University Press.

Asad, Talal (1986) 'The concept of cultural translation in British social anthropology'. In James Clifford and George E Marcus (eds) *Writing Culture: The Poetics and Politics of Ethnography.* Berkeley: University of California Press.

Attridge, Derek and David Attwell (eds) (2012) *The Cambridge History of South African Literature.* Cambridge: Cambridge University Press.

Attwell, David and JM Coetzee (1992) 'Interview'. In David Attwell (ed.) (1992) *Doubling the Point: Essays and Interviews.* Cambridge, MA/London: Harvard University Press.

Austin, JL (1986) (first published 1962) *How to Do Things with Words.* Oxford: Oxford University Press.

Bank, Andrew (2006) *Bushmen in a Victorian World: the Remarkable Story of the Bleek-Lloyd Collection of Bushman Folklore.* Cape Town: Double Storey.

Barnard, Rita (2009) 'Coetzee in/and Afrikaans', *Journal of Literary Studies,* 25(4) 84–105.

Bassnett, Susan (2002) *Translation Studies.* London: Routledge.

Biko, Nkosinathi (2000) 'Amnesty and Denial'. In Charles Villa-Vicencio and Wilhelm Verwoerd (eds) *Looking Forward, Reaching Back: Reflections on the Truth and Reconciliation Commission of South Africa.* Cape Town: UCT Press.

Boxer, CR (1990) (first published 1965). *The Dutch Sea-Borne Empire.* Harmondsworth: Penguin.

Boym, Svetlana (2001) *The Future of Nostalgia.* New York: Basic Books.

Brown, Duncan and Bruno van Dyk (1991) 'Interview with Njabulo Ndebele'. In *Exchanges: South African Writing in Transition.* Scottsville: University of Natal Press.

Casanova, Pascale (2009) 'Consecration and accumulation of literary capital: Translation as unequal exchange'. In Monica Baker (ed.) *Translation Studies* vol II, London: Routledge.

Coetzee, Carli (1994) 'Visions of disorder and profit: The Khoi and the first years of the Dutch East India Company at the Cape'. *Social Dynamics* 20(2): 35-66.

Coetzee, JM (1977) *In the Heart of the Country*. Johannesburg: Ravan.

Coetzee, JM (1988) *White Writing: On the Culture of Letters in South Africa*. New Haven and Cape Town: Yale University Press.

Coetzee, JM (1992) 'Jerusalem Acceptance Speech' (originally delivered in 1987). In David Attwell (ed.) (1992) *Doubling the Point: Essays and Interviews*. Cambridge, MA/London: Harvard University Press.

Coetzee, JM (1997) 'Their Man on Earth'. *New York Review of Books*, 6 March, 44(4). http://www.nybooks.com/articles/archives/1997/mar/06/their-man-on-earth/

Coetzee, JM (1999) *Disgrace*. London: Secker & Warburg.

Crystal, David (1991) (3rd edition). *A Dictionary of Linguistics and Phonetics*. Oxford: Basil Blackwell.

Davison, Patricia (1996) 'Foreword'. In *Miscast: Negotiating the Presence of the Bushmen*. Cape Town: UCT Press.

Diawara, Manthia (2009) (first published 1988) 'Black spectatorship: Problems of identification and resistance'. In Leo Braudy and Marshall Cohen (eds) (2009) (7th edition) *Film Theory and Criticism: Introductory Readings*. New York and Oxford: Oxford University Press.

Dlamini, Jacob. 2009. *Native Nostalgia*. Johannesburg: Jacana.

Duranti, Alessandro and Charles Goodwin (eds) (1992) *Rethinking Context: Language as an Interactive Phenomenon*. Cambridge: Cambridge University Press.

Egoyam, Atom and Ian Balfour (2004) *Subtitles: On the Foreignness of Film*. Boston: MIT Press.

Elphick, Richard (1985) *Khoikhoi and the Founding of White South Africa*. Braamfontein: Ravan.

Englehart, Lucinda (2003) 'Media activism in the screening room: The significance of viewing locations, facilitation and audience dynamics in the reception of HIV/AIDS films in South Africa'. *Visual Anthropology Review* 19(1/2), Spring-Summer: 73-85.

Enwezor, Okwui (1999) (first published 1997). 'Reframing the black subject: Ideology and fantasy in contemporary South African representation'. In Olu Oguibe and Okwui Enwezor (eds) *Reading the Contemporary: African Art from Theory to the Marketplace*. London: InIVA.

Fabian, Johannes (1983) *Time and the Other: How Anthropology Makes its Object*. New York: Columbia University Press.

Gallop, Jane (ed.) (1995) *Pedagogy: The Question of Impersonation*. Bloomington: Indiana University Press.

Gallop, Jane (2002) *Anecdotal Theory*. Durham: Duke University Press.

Gevisser, Mark (2009) *A Legacy of Liberation: Thabo Mbeki and the Future of the South African Dream*. New York: Palgrave Macmillan.

Gikandi, Simon (2000) 'Reading the referent: Postcolonialism and the writing of modernity'. In Susheila Nasta (ed.) *Reading the 'New' Literatures in a Postcolonial Era*. Cambridge: DS Brewer.

Goniwe, Thembinkosi (2006) 'Negotiating space: Some matters in South African contemporary art' (conference paper). In ED Ose (ed) *Erase Me From Who I Am: Catalogue of the Exhibition, Centro d'Atlántico De Arte Moderno*. Las Palmas de Gran Canaria.

Goniwe, Thembinkosi (2006) 'Targeted candidate, open letter to Emma Bedford', http://www.asai.co.za/word-view/opinion/item/58-targeted-candidate. html [Accessed 4 May 2012].

Gqola, Pumla (2010) *What is Slavery to Me? Postcolonial/Slave Memory in Post-Apartheid South Africa*. Johannesburg: Wits University Press.

Gunner, Liz, Dina Ligaga and Dumisani Moyo (2011) *Radio in Africa: Publics, Cultures, Communities*. Johannesburg: Witwatersrand University Press.

Hofmeyr, Isabel (2011) 'Foreword: Writing at sea'. In Delmas, Adrien and Nigel Penn (eds) (2011) *Written Culture in a Colonial Context: Africa and the Americas 1500-1900*. Cape Town: UCT Press.

Kasibe, Wandile Goozen (2006) 'Revisiting Identities/Positionalities in a Changing South African Socio-and Geopolitical Climate', paper delivered at the 'Race and Identity' Seminar held at the University of Cape Town, African Studies Gallery, on 7 September 2006.

Kasibe, Wandile Goozen (2006) 'Insides and outsides: Race and identity seminar' in *Monday Paper* Archives 25(19), 28 August 2006. www.uct.ac.za/print/mondaypeper/archives/?id-5873 [Accessed 16 June 2011].

Krog, Antjie (1998) *Country of my Skull*. Johannesburg: Random House.

Krog, Antjie (2003) *A Change of Tongue*. Johannesburg: Random House.

Krog, Antjie (2007) '… between the nose and the mouth. Perhaps more towards the eyes'. In Goldblatt, David (2007) *Some Afrikaners Revisited*. Cape Town: Umuzi.

Krog, Antjie (2009) *Begging to Be Black*. Johannesburg: Random House.

Krog, Antjie, Nosisi Mpolweni and Kopano Ratele (2009) *There was this Goat: Investigating the Truth Commission Testimony of Notrose Nobomvu Konile*. Scottsville: University of KwaZulu-Natal Press.

Leibbrandt, HCV (ed.) (1903) *Précis of the Archives of the Cape of Good Hope*. Cape Town: Richards.

Lekgoathi, Sekibakiba Peter (2011) 'Bantustan identity, censorship and subversion on Northern Sotho radio under apartheid, 1960s-80s'. In Gunner, Liz, Dina Ligaga and Dumisani Moyo (2011) *Radio in Africa: Publics, Cultures, Communities*. Johannesburg: Witwatersrand University Press.

Masilela, Ntongela (2004) 'Interview with Ntongela Masilela on the nature of the 'New African Movement website', by Sandile Ngidi. http://pzacad.pitzer.edu/NAM/general/conversation.pdf [Accessed 09 May 2012].

Masilela, Ntongela (n.d.) 'Issues in the historiography of South African literature', http://pzacad.pitzer.edu/nam/general/essays/issues.pdf [Accessed 22 March 2012].

Mesthrie, Rajend (2002) (ed.) *Language in South Africa*. Cambridge: Cambridge University Press.

Mesthrie, Rajend (2011) *Eish, but is it English?* Cape Town: Zebra Press.

Mokoena, Hlonipha (2011) *Magema Fuze: the Making of a Kholwa Intellectual.* Scottsville: University of KwaZulu-Natal Press.

Mphahlele, Es'kia (1983) 'South African literature vs the political morality'. *English Academy Review* 1(1): 8-28.

Mphahlele, Es'kia (1984) 'Prometheus in chains: The fate of English in South Africa'. *English Academy Review* 2(1): 89-104.

Mulvey, Laura (2009) (first published 1975) 'Visual pleasure and narrative cinema'. In Leo Braudy and Marshall Cohen (eds) (2009) (7th edition) *Film Theory and Criticism: Introductory Readings.* New York and Oxford: Oxford University Press.

Naficy, Hamid (2011) *An Accented Cinema: Exile and Diasporic Filmmaking.* Princeton and Oxford: Princeton University Press.

Ndebele, Njabulo (1983) *Fools and Other Stories.* Braamfontein: Ravan.

Ndebele, Njabulo (1987) 'The English language and social change in South Africa', *English Academy Review* 4(1): 1-16.

Ndebele, Njabulo (1991) *Rediscovery of the Ordinary: Essays on South African Literature and Culture.* Johannesburg: Cosaw.

Ndebele, Njabulo (1994) *South African Literature and Culture: Rediscovery of the Ordinary.* Manchester: Manchester University Press.

Ndebele, Njabulo (2003) *The Cry of Winnie Mandela, A Novel.* Banbury: Ayebia.

Ndebele, Njabulo (2006) *Rediscovery of the Ordinary: Essays on South African Literature and Culture.* Scottsville: University of KwaZulu Natal Press.

Ndebele, Njabulo (2007) *Fine Lines from the Box: Further Thoughts about Our Country.* Cape Town, Umuzi.

Ngũgĩ wa Thiong'o (1986) *Decolonising the Mind.* London: James Currey/ Heinemann.

Niranjana, Tejaswini (1992) *Siting Translation: History, Post-Structuralism, and the Colonial Context.* Berkeley: University of California Press.

Nuttall, Sarah (2009) *Entanglement.* Johannesburg: Wits University Press.

Péringuey, Louis Albert (1950) (3d edition, first published 1913) *Inscriptions Left by Early European Navigators on their Way to the East.* Cape Town: South African Museum.

Peterson, Bhekizizwe (2000) *Monarchs, Missionaries and African Intellectuals: African Theatre and the Unmaking of Colonial Marginality.* Trenton, NJ and Asmara: Africa World Press.

Posel, Deborah and Graeme Simpson (eds) (2002) *Commissioning the Past: Understanding the Truth and Reconciliation Commission.* Johannesburg: Wits University Press.

Raditlhalo, Tlhalo (2007) 'Assembling the broken gourds: An appreciation'. In Njabulo Ndebele (2007) *Fine Lines from the Box: Further Thoughts About our Country.* Cape Town: Umuzi.

Raditlhalo, Tlhalo (2012) 'Writing in Exile'. In Attridge, Derek and David Attwell (eds) (2012) *The Cambridge History of South African Literature.* Cambridge: Cambridge University Press.

Raven-Hart, R (1967) *Before Van Riebeeck: Callers at the Cape from 1488 to 1652.* Cape Town: Struik.

Ricard, Alain (2003) 'Africa and Writing'. In Irele, F Abiola and Simon Gikandi (2003) *The Cambridge History of African and Caribbean Literature* (Vol 1). Cambridge: Cambridge University Press.

Sachs, Albie (1991) 'Preparing ourselves for freedom: Culture and the ANC Constitutional Guidelines'. *The Drama Review* 35(1): 187-193.

Saks, Lucia (2010) *Cinema in a Democratic South Africa: The Race for Representation*. Bloomington and Indianapolis: Indiana University Press.

Samuelson, Meg (2007) *Remembering the Nation, Dismembering Women? Stories of the South African Transition*. Scottsville: University of KwaZulu-Natal Press.

Sanders, Mark (2007) *Ambiguities of Witnessing: Law and Literature in the Time of the Truth Commission*. Stanford: Stanford University Press.

Saunders, Walter, David Segatlhe and Benjamin Letholoa Leshoai (1990) (eds.) *Blue Black and Other Poems*. London: Hodder & Stoughton Educational.

Scott, James C (1990) *Domination and the Arts of Resistance: Hidden Transcripts*. New Haven: Yale University Press.

Skotnes, Pippa (1991) 'Rock art: Is there life after trance'. *De Arte 44*, September: 16-24.

Skotnes, Pippa (1991) *Sounds from the Thinking String: A Visual, Literary, Archaeological and Historical Interpretation of the Final Years of /Xam Life*. Cape Town: Axeage Private Press.

Skotnes, Pippa (1996) 'The thin black line: Diversity and transformation in the Bleek and Lloyd Collection and the paintings of the Southern San'. In Deacon, Janette and Thomas A Dowson (eds.) *Voices from the Past: /Xam Bushmen and the Bleek and Lloyd Collection*. Johannesburg: Wits University Press.

Skotnes, Pippa (2007) (ed.) *Claim to the Country: The Archive of Wilhelm Bleek and Lucy Lloyd*. Johannesburg: Jacana.

Skotnes, Pippa (2009) *The Unconquerable Spirit: George Stow's History Paintings of the San*. Johannesburg: Jacana.

Skotnes, Pippa (2011) *Rock Art: Made in Translation. Framing Images of and from the Landscape*. Johannesburg: Jacana.

Skotnes, Pippa (n.d.) *The digital Bleek and Lloyd*. www.lloydbleekcollection. cs.uct.ac.za/ [Accessed 11 May 2012].

Smith, Candice (2000) (ed.) *Returning the Gaze: Public Arts Project at the Cape Town One City Festival 2001*. Cape Town: BLAC.

Stadler, Jane (2003) 'Narrative, understanding and identification in Steps for the Future HIV/AIDS documentaries'. *Visual Anthropology Review* 19(1/2), Spring-Summer: 86-101.

Steinberg, Jonny (2008) *Sizwe's Test: A Young Man's Journey Through Africa's AIDS Epidemic*. New York: Simon & Schuster.

Steinberg, Jonny (2009) (first published 2008) *Three Letter Plague*. London: Vintage.

Twidle, Hedley (2010) 'Prison and Garden: Cape Town, Natural History and the Literary Imagination'. PhD Thesis. University of York.

Twidle, Hedley (2012) 'The Bushmen's Letters: /Xam narratives of the Bleek and Lloyd Collection and their Afterlives'. In Attridge, Derek and David Attwell (eds.) (2012) *The Cambridge History of South African Literature*. Cambridge: Cambridge University Press.

Van der Vlies, Andrew (2010) *Disgrace: A Reader's Guide*. London: Continuum.

Van der Watt, Liese (2003) 'The Many Hearts of Whiteness: Dis-investing in Whiteness Through South African Visual Culture'. PhD Thesis, State University of New York.

Wainaina, Binyavanga (2011) *One Day I Will Write About This Place*. London: Granta.

Wicomb, Zoë (2001) *David's Story*. New York: The Feminist Press.

Wicomb, Zoë (2005) 'Setting, intertextuality and the resurrection of the postcolonial author'. *Journal of Postcolonial Writing* 41(2): 144-55.

Wicomb, Zoë (2008) *The One That Got Away*. Cape Town: Umuzi.

Wicomb, Zoë (2008) Zoë Wicomb at the Dundee Literary Salons. http://vimeo.com/5230553 [Accessed 11 May 2012].

Willemse, Hein (2002) 'Zoë Wicomb in Conversation with Hein Willemse'. *Research in African Literatures* 33(1): 144-52.

Wilson, Richard (2001) *The Politics of Truth and Reconciliation in South Africa*, Cambridge: Cambridge University Press.

Worden, Nigel (ed.) (2007) 'New approaches to VOC history in South Africa'. *South African Historical Journal* 59: 3-18.

Index